I0186970

LUMMOX Press

Working the Wreckage of the American Poem

A Smoky Memory of Todd Moore
by some of his fans

Edited by RD Armstrong

LUMMOX Press

Working the Wreckage of the American Poem

©2011 by RD Armstrong (editor)

All rights reserved. No part of this book may be reproduced without express written permission from the editor, except for the purposes of review.

ISBN 978-1-929878-93-2

LUMMOX Press
PO Box 5301
San Pedro, CA 90733

www.lummoxpress.com

Printed in the USA

Working the
Wreckage
of the
American Poem

TABLE OF CONTENTS

RD ARMSTRONG
Long Beach, CA

AN INTRODUCTION

TODD MOORE wrote about blood and bone, about death and darkness...he was always deconstructing and reassembling the world around him; concentrating on what he knew best and for thirty-five years, using the metaphor of the mythic outlaw, John Dillinger, to explain his vision of America. Dillinger was a wonderful vehicle for Todd: rough and tumble; a wild ride down a dirt road in the dead of night...an unknown character from the past, a simple canvas on which Todd could paint his imaginary world. But it wasn't just a world of cops and robbers, though it may have started out that way. By the time Todd died, that imaginary world had become a multi-faceted, multi-dimensional land of wonder full of shamans and voodoo, gangsters and low-lifes...it was ALIVE and scary, just like what Todd had always imagined was going on out there, beyond the light, where the dark things creep and plot their revenge.

I first met Todd Moore in 2000 in Albuquerque, NM or ABQ as some call it. Here is an excerpt from the poem that I wrote (On/Off the Beaten Path) about the whole trip. This part details my first encounter with Todd:

> *I pictured Todd and wife Barbara*
> *living in a nice little pueblo-style*
> *two bedroom adobe job on San*
> *Pedro Street*
> *(sounds pretty rustic right?)*
> *Not so.*

Strictly suburban daddy-o.
Unassuming and anonymous
I drove by it twice.
No one would ever suspect
that the guy who wrote
The Corpse is Dreaming
lived there and ate there
and worked out the crazy
catechism that is "Sundance":
a mixture of knives
literature and leather-tough
characters from his past.
Sundance writes THE POEM –
it's raw and ragged and sometimes
it won't stop bleeding...
It bleeds because at its core
all his poems have a heart
(a heart that must pump because
that's what hearts do – pump – other
wise a heart is just a pound of meat).
So – of course – I expect Sundance
to have that air of machismo
that one sees swaggering around the El Lay
Western hangouts.
No dice pilgrim.
Sundance is a quiet guy who
speaks intensely about THE POEM
who bristles when he thinks about
those who pretend and practice at
the craft...

And that was my first meeting with the man who had already had a major influence with both my writing as well as the way I lived my life. To some degree Todd was more mentor than friend. At times, I could almost mistake him for my peer and I hate to admit it but sometimes I hoped he might take me under his wing. But I was too old for such behavior and not as talented as the numerous other poets who sought Todd's counsel.

Don't get me wrong, I loved him as much as my own father.

Now it is many years later and I have grown in so many ways. Todd is no longer moving amongst us. He rests quietly in Northern Illinois, the cool earth embracing him, protecting him from all the BS that holds our lives together. Todd sleeps the big sleep, perhaps dreaming of another section of the Dillinger saga, his epic poem that refused to end...Todd wrote the *last* chapter, The Corpse is Dreaming, in 1999, but added many more sections to that before he was done.

What follows here is the work of numerous writers & poets. Each has his or her own connection to Todd, which is demonstrated by their contribution. Some have written essays, some remembrances, most have written poems. Not every contributor has a positive view of Todd's contribution, but I think in order to present Todd's effect on the world of small press poetry, one must present the view of both his detractors as well as supporters. And I think it's safe to say that they all miss him in their own way. I know I do.

I hope that you, the reader, will find this collection of voices of interest (perhaps an introduction to some of the most interesting and provocative voices in the small press today).

I miss you Todd.

Todd Moore at a reading in Berkeley in May, 2009
Photo by Roy Manzanares

TONY MOFFEIT
Pueblo, CO

THE FASTEST GUN IN THE WEST

TODD MOORE died on March 12, 2010. Todd Moore was an outlaw. Todd Moore was about speed. Todd Moore lived in Albuquerque, New Mexico. Todd Moore was the fastest gun in the West. Todd Moore shot word bullets. Todd Moore burned with velocity, burned with ferocity, burned with the blood. Todd Moore was about velocity and the visceral, speed and the physical. There were not enough minutes in the day for Todd Moore. And when he finally slept, he continued his outlaw monologues and dialogues in his dreams. Todd Moore was the fastest gun in the West. Outlaw is about speed. The speed of getting the words down on paper. The speed of innovation. The speed of revolutionizing the short poem. Todd Moore revolutionized the short poem. His style of the short poem with a wallop, the short poem with an ironic violence, the short poem with a machine gun velocity influenced generations of poets. Todd Moore revolutionized the long poem. His masterpiece, DILLINGER, was a raw, lyrical, poem-movie that splashed across the page in waves of violence, or knifed across the page in a stiletto-like condensed line, stabbing out words and phrases. Todd Moore revolutionized the essay. His essays combined autobiographical prose, poetry, literary criticism, and outlaw philosophy to yield a whole new approach and lyricism to the essay. Todd Moore was the fastest gun in the West.

Outlaw is about creating yourself out of nothing. Todd Moore created his literary persona out of growing up in the Clifton Hotel, his obsession with going to movies, and his fascination with the legend of John Dillinger. His most personal writing, the writing in which you most got to know Todd Moore, came about in the essays he wrote later in his life. Todd Moore had stories to tell, and the story of Todd Moore was told in these essays. Todd Moore was the fastest gun in the West. Outlaw is about being an individual who creates one's own laws and outlaw is about being a ghost. The other half of outlaw is ghost. The other half of ghost is outlaw. Many of Todd Moore's characters were phantom shapeshifters and Todd Moore himself was a ghost. Todd Moore was about the body, the blood, the physical. And Todd Moore was about pure energy, the velocity of a superb and blinding force. Todd Moore was the burning of pure energy. Todd Moore was a blaze of pure energy. Todd Moore was a pure example of speed. Todd Moore was a lightning flash. Todd Moore was the fastest gun in the West. Todd Moore was a pure example of constant creativity. His condensed line was speaking in a subatomic level, innovative, inventive. He was pure force. His work was an electrical power plant. His work was a theory of relativity of poetry. His work was a nuclear force of a new kind of poem, a new kind of essay. He was himself an infinite flux of energy that he was constantly creating.

Todd Moore's poem was a gun. Todd Moore's words were bullets. Todd Moore left blood on the page. Todd Moore was the fastest gun in the West. Todd Moore was in a constant gunfight with death. And he knew the only way to outdraw death was to transcend death through language. It's a hard bullet. It's a word bullet. That bullet talks so fast. Todd Moore was the fastest gun in the West. Todd Moore was always in flux. Todd Moore was about the flesh of dreams, dreams with good red blood. Todd Moore was about the intensity of creativity and the invisibility of disappearance. Todd Moore was the fastest gun in the West.

Outlaw is about the very essence of existence: how you think your thoughts, how you create your thoughts, how you invent your ideas, how you come to some sort of newfound creativity, how you attain ecstasy in the midst of chaos, how you attain calm in the middle of chaos, how you attain chaos in the middle of calm. Outlaw is about changing your life by not changing your life. Outlaw is a Zen puzzle. Outlaw is quantum physics played out in the most simple and direct everyday gestures and ideas. How is a person's life measured? By the immeasurable. Where is substance? In void.

Todd Moore died at the very height of his creative powers. He had always been productive, but in the months and years prior to his death he reached a new level of creativity, a new level of language. He was a flame, a blaze, a fire. Todd Moore was the fastest gun in the West. Spring had arrived with a mad Dillinger moon. The machine gun night was shooting stars into the sky over the mountains. Spring had arrived with a cosmic trickster joke. Todd Moore left in the middle of his greatest binge of word bullets of them all. Todd Moore was the fastest gun in the West.

Todd Moore had the amazing ability to write spontaneous poems whenever he had a spare five minutes or so to capture some outlaw words. In a restaurant, at a poetry reading, between appointments, if there was a space for writing, Todd Moore could feel the rush of creativity and improvise a poem on the spot. He was the fastest gun in the West. Not only would he create a poem, but if a poet friend was nearby, he would share the poem. Poetry readings were often not only a place to read poems, but were also a place to write poems. It was as if there were always poems in the air and he was going to capture them. Todd Moore was the fastest gun in the West.

Todd Moore had the competitive fire of a great athlete. Todd Moore was one of those rare individuals with the burning desire to be number one. He wanted to be the best. He wanted to be the fastest gun in the West. And so he wrote and wrote and wrote and wrote. He reminded me of something Arlo Guthrie told me about his father, Woody. I asked him to describe his father to me. And he did. In one sentence: "He'd rather write than eat." Todd Moore had the astonishing capacity to jump from one level to another in his writings, building, evolving, creating, inventing, working on many levels at one time. The innovation and stimulation of ideas were invigorating. He was the fastest gun in the West.

When I think of the roots of outlaw, I think of those who created a new level of consciousness through self-expression, through self-creation. I think of those who created their own laws. Where does the outlaw get his power? From himself. Where did Todd Moore get his power? From himself. He was the fastest gun in the West. The purpose of outlaw is to identify the unidentifiable, to define the indefinable, to categorize the uncategorizable. The outlaw is a ghost. The outlaw is a ghost who carries the speed of invisibility. Todd Moore was a ghost who carried the speed of invisibility. He was the fastest gun in the West.

Out of a barren landscape comes the outlaw. One lone figure on the horizon. Then another. Then another. Returning like the buffalo. Walking alone like the buffalo. Making himself out of nothing. Creating himself out of nothing but the fire in his blood. He is the one with no name. He now has a name. He is the one with no identity. He now has an identity. He is the one with no face. He now has a face. He is the one with no voice. He now has a voice. The best spirit found in the flesh of his sound. He is the fastest gun in the West.

* * *

INSIDE THE OUTLAW: AN INTERVIEW OF TONY MOFFEIT BY *ORION*

Tony Moffeit is the award winning blues poet/musician/ artist from Pueblo, Colorado. For the last three and a half decades he has been churning out an extraordinarily unique style of poetry, music, and visual art.

In 2004 Tony Moffeit and Todd Moore founded the outlaw movement in poetry. With the death of Todd Moore on March 12, 2010, Tony Moffeit gave his thoughts on the Outlaw Poetry Movement, and "Moore."

INTERVIEW

Orion: Hi, Tony. Thanks for sitting down with us today. How are you?

Tony Moffeit: I'm fine, but still stunned by the sudden death of Todd Moore.

O: I understand. My condolences go out to you and all the others who knew and loved Todd.

TM: I had never seen anyone burn with the creative passion of Todd Moore in the years prior to his death. He had always been productive, but he reached another level of creative energy in those years and went out in a flame, a blaze, a fire.

O: I agree. I love his Riddle of the Wooden Gun. Tony, you've been writing a brand of poetry for quite some time...completely unique and different from anyone... You've some 30 some books filled with wild, romantic, rustic, and surreal poetry. How on earth did you discover such a diamond mine?

TM: I'm glad you asked me about my writing in terms of discovering a diamond mine, because in so many ways, the poems are discovered, revealed, uncovered, unveiled. In many ways, the poems are writing me, as much as I am writing the poems. But the main thing, I believe, is creating a persona, an individual poetic identity, or more than that, personas, identities. Once you are in that poetic character, the poems almost write themselves. That character might be myself traveling through the Southwest, or it may be myself visiting New Orleans. It might be blues poet, outlaw poet, or I might take on other identities, like a voodoo king, as in my poem, "luminous animal."

The other side of the coin, however, is dissolving your identity, so that you become a ghost, and your poems become a kind of ghost language.

O: Would you like to elaborate on the latter, "dissolving your identity, becoming a ghost..." Is that like becoming a part of the environment, a hallucinogenic part of the landscape so well depicted in your work?

TM: It's closer to getting in touch with mystical forces. It's like becoming a receptor to mystical forces, allowing yourself to become a channel for mystical or universal or invisible forces. As well as creating a new identity, a poetic identity, it is also important to dissolve your identity, in order to become a receptor to universal forces. A method for doing this: find a particular mystical place, which for me is Taos, New Mexico. Check into the Adobe Wall Motel, right down the road from the San Geronimo Pueblo. And in the adobe darkness, turn out all the lights, and in the dark, scribble the poems down as you fluctuate between sleep and waking. Write for hours in the darkness. Then transcribe the scribbles the next day in the light. Once at a poetry reading in Denver I described this method of writing in the dark. The poet Scarecrow quipped, "Hey, we never knew that you ever wrote in the light."

O: You've definitely found a path worth following in and of itself, your very own...and perhaps for others too!

You've also done quite a bit of research as well, much of which is documented in the essays included in your book, *Poetry Is Dangerous, The Poet Is An Outlaw*. For instance, you spoke of Henry Miller, D.H. Lawrence, the Surrealists, etc. So...you put those in a pot, season, bring to a boil and pour out all over the west, and you get Tony Moffeit! It's so magical, enchanting, perfect...is there anything else to it? Are there any more secrets you would like to share thus far down the pike and twenty years or so after the release of those essays?

TM: The book *Poetry Is Dangerous, The Poet Is An Outlaw* introduced the outlaw essay. My outlaw essays have continued, primarily through two outlaw websites, *metropolis* in Paris, France and *st. vitus press and poetry review* in Albuquerque, New Mexico. The ideas in the essays in *Poetry Is Dangerous, The Poet Is An Outlaw* have been expanded and developed. I would like to discuss a couple of the ideas in relation to Todd Moore.

One of the central meanings to the phrase "poetry is dangerous, the poet is an outlaw" is that for the outlaw poet, poetry is more than just writing poetry, it is a way of life. Externally, the outlaw poet may be no different from anyone else. But internally he is a revolutionary, an innovator, a creator of new myths, new metaphors, new archetypes. Poetry is dangerous because the poet is obsessed with following his own way, and following the path which his art takes him. This means a lot of separateness, a lot of independence, an endless search for self, an endless creativity. The path is all-consuming. He lives on the edge. He burns on the edge. Todd Moore is a good example of this. He was absolutely on fire, to the very end. In his early 70s he had the will, passion, and energy of someone fifty years younger. He knew no other way than to be totally consumed by his art.

A related phrase is "to live inside the poem is to be an outlaw." It goes along with "poetry is dangerous, the poet is an outlaw." The outlaw poet believes that you create who you are. The outlaw poet believes you are who you create yourself to be. The outlaw poet believes that you make your life a work of art. At the same time, you make your art a work of life. Your art comes alive through the overflow of intensified life experience. Todd Moore lived for the next poem. It's what made him tick. He lived inside his next poem. His identity was wrapped up in his next poem, his next essay, his next piece of autobiographical prose. Communicating with him on almost a daily level for more than ten years via email was to feel the excitement of someone who couldn't wait to get to the next idea, the next poem, the next essay, the next metaphor. Todd Moore was not completely happy unless he was living inside his next piece of work.

O: In 2004, you and Todd started the Outlaw Poetry

Movement, a natural extension of this thought. You also did an interview with Mark Weber in 1995, published in *Chiron Review*, and an interview with Raindog in 2000, published in *Lummox*, where you touched on the artist as individual and outlaw. Who is the outlaw?

TM: Well, that is the question. The question is: Who is the outlaw? On the most simple level, I want to break down the word into its two parts, its two syllables. The first part, or syllable, "out" describes the outlaw in this way: the outlaw is out on the side. He is separate. He is individualistic. He is independent. He follows his own way because he knows no other way than his own. There is no other way than his own. He is different. He is unique. He is self-sufficient. He is out there on the side, in a different realm, a mysterious realm, a realm of a world that is all his own. The other half of the word is "law," as in a law unto yourself. The outlaw is that individual who creates one's own laws. The outlaw is the one who creates oneself. The outlaw is the one who makes his life a work of art. The outlaw is about self-creation. The outlaw is the one who lives his life in an innovative way. The outlaw is the one who creates his own artistic identity.

Now let's put the two parts of the word back together again. Who is the outlaw? The outlaw is that individual who is thrown back on himself, who has nothing left but himself, who has denied all else, who has reached rock bottom in order to begin to create something new: his own identity. And, through his own identity, his own art. The outlaw is that individual who creates one's own laws. The outlaw is that individual who is a law unto oneself. The outlaw is that individual who creates oneself. The outlaw is that individual who in the process of creating oneself, creates one's own art. Who is it? Outlaw. What is it? Outlaw. How do you recognize him? He is the one who is a law unto oneself. How do you recognize it? It is a law unto itself. What do you call him? Outlaw. What do you call it? Outlaw. What is his nature? Out of nothing, to create himself. What is its nature? Out of nothing, to create itself. What is the product? Innovation in identity. What is the product? Innovation in art. What is the product? Innovation in thought. What is the product? Innovation in ideas. What is the product? Creating something new. What is the product? Revolution. What is the product? A change in consciousness.

O: As long as it is "fully what we believe" as you said in your essays, right?

TM: You bring up an important point. Unless you fully believe that you can create your own life, your own art, your own world, unless you fully believe that you can create your own consciousness, then you are back into a kind of conditioning which tells you that you are created by something else, which tells you that you are controlled by the external world. A basic idea of outlaw is "the internal world of the outlaw, the creative world of the outlaw is superior to the external world." In other words, the creative consciousness of the individual is more powerful than external forces. If this idea is transformed into a belief then that is an important step to creative power. This idea is very close to the idea that quantum physics gives us. Quantum physics tells us that matter and energy only exist when there is a consciousness to observe them. In other words, consciousness creates the universe. If you carry this forward to an outlaw idea, then we are nothing more than what we create ourselves to be through our own consciousness. You create the reality which you experience.

O: And, as Willie Nelson says, "Be careful what you're

dreaming, because soon your dreams will be dreaming you!"

TM: Yes, that statement of Willie Nelson's is a deeply philosophical statement that also corresponds to some of the ideas of quantum physics and, of course, to some of the ideas of outlaw. I'm talking about the nature of reality. Yesterday I was watching a video on YouTube on quantum physics when a person came on the screen saying, "There is no such thing as death. Life is only a dream and we are the imagination of ourselves." Again, the only reality we really know is that which is manufactured by our consciousness. So, thank you for that Willie Nelson line. A related idea is that everything we think and everything we do has an impact on our lives, on what we are creating. It is as if we are constantly creating self-fulfilling prophecies.

O: And thank you for getting to the bottom of that! I just love your last sentence.

TM: I appreciate that. On another level, I want to tell you about a dream that my guitarist, Rick Terlep, had about Todd Moore, after Todd's death. In Rick's dream, Todd Moore is dreaming, and in Todd's dream he is in a theater, and the people in the theater look familiar, but he can't quite place them. Also, there is a woman in the seat beside him and she also looks familiar, but he can't quite place her. Finally, the movie ends, and he is walking out of the theater when someone calls to him "John!" and he turns around because he now recognizes who he is and he sees in the reflection of a mirror the words "Biograph Theater."

O: Who were the first outlaws?

TM: In Western culture, the German philosopher,

Friedrich Nietzsche. Nietzsche felt that the individual was justification in himself, meaning in himself. That is outlaw. Nietzsche felt that one goes into the desert of himself to recognize who he is, and more than that, to create who he is. That is outlaw. Nietzsche called this self-overcoming the will to power. That is outlaw. Nietzsche created new personas for himself: the Overman or Superman and Zarathustra. That is outlaw. Nietzsche's greatest philosophical work was a work of poetry: *Thus Spake Zarathustra*. That is outlaw. Nietzsche felt that one should create one's own philosophy. That is outlaw. One should create one's own power. That is outlaw. One should create one's own ideas. That is outlaw. How should one do that? Through one's own poetry. Through one's own essays. Through one's own prose. That is outlaw. Nietzsche felt that the outlaw is defined by his love of his own life. That is outlaw. Nietzsche felt that the true justification of this love of one's own life was not heaven, but eternal recurrence in the earth itself: to live one's own life over and over again. To create oneself over and over again is the ultimate goal. That is outlaw.

The first outlaw in Eastern culture was the founder of Zen Buddhism, Bodhidharma, who traveled from India to China with a secret doctrine, carried by himself, Zen. In China, when he was met by an emperor, and given an audience, the emperor told Bodhidharma that he had built great temples, educated monks and nuns, and copied holy scriptures. Then he asked Bodhidharma if there was any merit in what he had done. "No merit whatsoever," answered Bodhidharma. That is outlaw. The emperor, taken aback, asked, "What, then, is the holy truth, the first principle?" Bodhidharma answered, "In vast emptiness, there is nothing holy." "Who then are you to stand before me?" asked the emperor. "I know not," answered Bodhidharma and walked away. That is outlaw. Outlaw is not about external power. Outlaw is about internal power. Bodhidharma was well known for contemplating the wall of a cave. His first disciple, Huike, approached him for an audience. Bodhidharma did not answer. Huike waited outside the cave in the snow for a week. Bodhidharma would still not give him an audience. Finally, the disciple cut off his left arm to show his seriousness and presented it to Bodhidharma. That is outlaw. However, Bodhidharma didn't want his arm. He wanted his mind. Huike said, "I have no peace of mind. Can you pacify my mind?" Bodhidharma replied, "Bring your mind before me and I will pacify it." Huike said, "I have searched and searched but I cannot find my mind." Bodhidharma replied, "There! I have pacified your mind!" Huike was enlightened and became Bodhidharma's spiritual successor. That is outlaw. Searching and searching and searching for your own mind.

So if you want to go to the first outlaws, go to those who invented their own philosophy, their own religion. Go to those who abandoned all else to create themselves. Go to those who abandoned all else to create their own art, their own ideas, their own thought. What are the traits of the outlaw? He walks alone. Nietzsche and Bodhidharma are two of the most solitary and mysterious individuals in the history of thought. The outlaw is madly in love with life. So madly in love with life, thought Nietzsche, that his greatest wish would be to live one's own life over and over again. The outlaw brings a change in consciousness. For Bodhidharma, this change in consciousness was identified as sudden enlightenment.

The outlaw's primary communication is with other outlaws, and preferably one on one. The outlaw generally begins with nothingness, a void, through which he creates himself. He wants that barren landscape, that marginality, in order to give meaning to it. Who is he? He is who he is. Who is he? He is who he is not. Who is he? He is the ghost who has left himself. When is he most himself? When he is least himself, when he is the ghost of himself. How does he find himself? By losing himself. What is the language he uses? Ghost language. How does he write his poems? By allowing the poems to write themselves. What is he? Outlaw and ghost. What is the other half of outlaw? Ghost. What is the other half of ghost? Outlaw. How do you recognize him? In his invisibility. How do you recognize him? In his marginality. Where does he live? In a barren landscape. Where does he live? Inside his own poem. Being an outlaw means living out on the side.

O: Who are other outlaws?

TM: The poet Jack Micheline was an outlaw. He was an outlaw in his independent lifestyle. He went his own way. He certainly fit the criterion of marginality, for he called himself a street poet, living vicariously on the streets of New York and San Francisco, in and out of hotels and rooms provided by friends. He was always on the move. Also, in his poetry, his essays, his interviews, and his performances he was defining an outlaw way that was individualistic and at the same time, lyrical. In 1964, he edited an anthology called *Six American Poets* and in an introductory essay to the volume he wrote: "To be a real poet is to be a part of the waves of the sea. To give freely, asking no reward. To be a star that shines bright in a dark sky. Sometimes the tides hurl his body against the rocks, but somehow he keeps on going, carrying some blind faith within him. He stands alone amidst our frightened ages, using his eyes as a mirror. Somehow, by some miracle he survives."

The poet d.a. levy was an outlaw. If Jack Micheline

was Nietzsche, d.a. levy was Bodhidharma. He had a strong sense of the void and that language which defines the outlaw: ghost language. d.a. levy realized that you are who you are. And you are who you are not. You are a will and a receptacle; you are a force and you are a receptor, a vessel through which mystical forces run. You allow the poem to write you as much as you write the poem. Here are some words of d.a. levy, from the poem "Tombstone As A Lonely Charm": "whenever you get bored/change headlines/colors politics words/change women/but if you really want/a revolution/learn how to change/your internal chemistry/then go beyond that/walk down the streets/& flash lights/at yourself"

O: While magnifying a new genre in poetry, you also seem to be giving the definition of outlaw a new meaning, or taking it back to its origins. It's almost as though there is a shamanistic (trance/healing) element that must be present in the outlaw's art, which when effective often becomes mainstream sensation once it's recognized by the culture at large. Is there a social diagnosis/prescription from the outlaw?

TM: Right at the core of outlaw is the question, "Who am I?" or "What am I?" And the outlaw answers, "I am who I create myself to be." Or: I am that individual who I create myself to be. Or: I am that unique and independent individual who I create myself to be. Or: I am that consciousness that I create myself to be. Outlaw is about being a law unto yourself. Outlaw is about being an independent individual. Outlaw is about being a new form of consciousness which you create.

So, right at the crux of outlaw is that primary philosophical question, "Who am I?" Right at the crux of outlaw is that search for self, that search for different ways of inventing the self. One of the basic tenets of Zen is the following:

> *a special transmission outside the scriptures*
> *no dependence on words and letters*
> *direct pointing to the mind of man*
> *seeing into one's own nature*

Again, "seeing into one's own nature" is crucial to that independent individual called the outlaw. The first step to creating and the first step to healing is to know who you are and who you want to create yourself to be.

Like the shaman, the outlaw is interested in the secret energies in the universe. Besides "Who am I?" the outlaw wants to know "Where am I?" or "What is the nature of the universe?" Nietzsche felt that there were two basic forces in the universe: the will to power and the emotion of fear. After further reflection, he intuited that the emotion of fear was simply a lack of the will to power. So, he thought, there was only one basic force in the universe: the will to power. In outlaw terms, there are two basic forces in the universe: self-creation and the conditioning of the external world. The conditioning of the external world is simply a lack of self-creation. So, the basic force in the universe is self-creation.

Quantum physics gives us the idea that nothing can be measured without a measurer. Nothing exists in the universe without an observer to observe it. In other words, consciousness creates everything. Without consciousness, the universe is a blob, a mass of matter and energy without meaning or even existence. At the same time, everything, from the ant to the galaxies is made of the same material, atoms and subatomic particles. So, everything is interconnected, everything is entangled.

So, we have two truths about the nature of reality, the nature of existence. One is that consciousness creates everything. The other is that everything is interconnected, interrelated.

So, what does outlaw have to offer in terms of the way you live your life? It offers a recognition and a challenge to two of the basic questions of existence, "Who am I?" and "What is the nature of the universe?" Once those questions are answered individually by a person, then there is the potential for transformation.

What else does outlaw have to offer in terms of the way you live your life? To answer that, one must ask what is the goal, the meaning, the most health-related aspect of life? And the outlaw's answer to this is that it is whatever makes one more madly in love with life, whatever makes one more revitalized with living, whatever makes one more charged with ecstatic energy in the here and now.

Now in terms of concrete examples of this idea, I want to talk about a conference I attended on the Beats in Cherry Valley, New York, in 1998. One of the featured poets was a poet I had admired for a number of years, Ray Bremser. He had on a great hat, an Australian cowboy hat, and I told him I wanted his hat. He gave it to me and it is still one of my treasures. The conference lasted three days and Ray was there for four nights and he was not only a poet, he was an outlaw force. Although ill and in and out of hospitals, he was going nonstop, telling stories, telling about his dreams, constantly quoting his own poetry, reading new poems, telling about the experiences of his life. He was on fire. The poets who roomed with him said they could not get any sleep. He was up all night wanting to talk. And his poetry readings at the conference were amazing. But even more amazing was my first meeting of Ray Bremser in the front yard of Charles Plymell's stone house in Cherry Valley. Ray, as soon as he met me, felt like I was a brother. And he pulled me aside, to a vacant part of the lawn and said, "I want to tell you a secret. You wanta know a secret?" I laughed and said yeah. "Well," he said, "The secret to life is learning to love *everything*." Then, because he had been in and out of hospitals, he repeated the message, "The secret of life is to learn to love *everything*: even *hospitals*! Ray Bremser died in a hospital a few months later, but for three days and four nights, he was more than alive, he was immortal.

At the Beat conference in Cherry Valley, I didn't think it could get any better than my first conversation with Ray Bremser. But it did. It got even better. I walked inside Charles Plymell's stone house and the music was blasting with the blues: the unbelievable rhythms and shouts of Elmore James! And in the center of the living room was Charles Plymell, in a hipster zoot suit, doing the most electric dance I had ever seen: the energy was incomparable. And everyone who entered the house had to dance! Dance by themselves! And yet even though everyone was dancing by themselves the energy was being transferred from one individual to another: it was the supreme outlaw experience of universality, led by the pied piper of outlaws, Charles Plymell.

What else does outlaw have to offer in terms of the way one lives one's life? It has to do with language. And language as the entry way into the shamanic and the mystical through the wavelength of words. It has to do with language being a crevice of light into the void, changing one's consciousness. The best of the outlaw poems and essays change everything. They change the way you think. They change your perception of things.

They are lightning charges of a new reality. They are creations of a new reality.

Outlaw is about the recognition of a new reality. What is this new reality called? Outlaw. It is a new reality because it is about lawlessness. It is about the invention of your own laws. At the same time, the outlaw touches a universality, a totality in which all is one, one is all. Who are you? You are me. Who am I? I am you. What is it? To be the me that is you the you that is me.

O: What is another one of your experiences with an outlaw poet?

TM: Also in 1998, I phoned Jack Micheline because I needed some new poetry of his. He was living in a hotel in San Francisco. He said "Send me $200 cash and I'll send you something you'll really like." I sent him the $200 and he sent me an original manuscript, a book he made up himself, poetry with some original artwork, the only copy of it, which is invaluable. He wrote out, "Copy #1 of One copy," and signed the homemade volume. But even more important, he told me, "Hey, you've gotta come out to San Francisco. There's this street musician. He plays blues harmonica. We've gotta track him down and have him play blues harp behind our poetry!" I couldn't get away but I should have. I'll always regret not traveling to San Francisco immediately and searching out the blues harmonica player. What an adventure that would have been! A few months later, Jack Micheline died on a train, the San Francisco public transit system called the BART.

O: I imagine you have had a lot of unique experiences, tell us about Todd Moore.

TM: To talk about Todd Moore is always to give an

example of what outlaw is all about. Outlaw is about a new level of consciousness, a new level of burning intensity. And nobody burned like Todd Moore. He had that obsessive fire of the outlaw. And it was found through the visceral, the blood, the body, a revitalizing energy. I'm talking about burning on a daily level. There were not enough hours in the day. And his writing just got better and better and better. He revolutionized the short poem. Then he revolutionized the long poem. And then he revolutionized the essay. His essays were part essay, part poetry, part autobiographical prose, just nothing like you've ever seen before. And always there was the visceral, the blood, the body. The most often asked question of Todd Moore was why the fascination with Dillinger, why the fascination with violence? Todd addressed this time and time again in his own interviews, but I'll give you my take on it. The outlaw is recognized through his freedom, his independence, his wildness. The outlaw breaks out of established patterns, expected behavior. Order and organization are crucial to existence, but equally crucial are chaos, passion, and self-creation. The wildness and passion of the outlaw are vital to the balance necessary for the fullness of life, the totality of existence. Reaching a blood level of language was crucial for Todd. And the essence of the visceral was found in violence. He wanted the words to erupt volcano-like off the page. He was about intensity and he found the greatest intensity in writing about Dillinger, Baby Face Nelson, childhood experiences, and the outlaw. He was also about speed, the velocity of language, the velocity of writing. He was amazing. I would be just about finished looking at a new work of his, and he would already have sent another new work via email for me to look at. I loved the obsessiveness of this outlaw. I loved the compulsiveness of this outlaw. Because there were no limits with Todd, there were no stops to take a breath with Todd, it was all go, go, go. He was amazingly productive, but more than that was the intensity with which he wrote. And he was never satisfied. He was looking for more intensity, more machine gun language, more ways to get the words to leap off the page. And so Todd transferred this incredible energy, this magnificent life force on a daily level. He transferred the innovation of ideas on a daily level. He transferred the invention of new archetypes, new metaphors, new symbols on a daily level. And he went out at the peak of his creative powers. He died at the peak of his creativity.

Todd Moore, Tony Moffeit & Lawrence Welsh

HUGH FOX
E. Lansing, MI

I GET A LETTER from my pal, A.D. Winans, in San Francisco, that Todd Moore just died. Ah, for crissake! And then the next day tons of letters about the same death. And for the last twenty years I've had this poem of his in front of my work-desk, framed, next to the poem a little line-drawing of a guy shooting a gun at another guy, under it hand-written: "running away from the same goddam thing that waits just ahead." And next to it: "For Hugh Fox, 6/14/91." Nineteen years. And me just a month after my 78th birthday.

It's too much. Back in the old COSMEP-Hippy days we were all like one big family. Then my pal Bukowski died, not long after I'd written a book about him during the ten years I was in L.A.., then Richard Morris, Curt Johnson in Highland Park, Illinois, Carol Berge, William Wantling, Dick Higgins......the walls of my workroom filled with signed poem-samples from all the old gang. A lot of them still around, Potts and Krech, Robert Bly, Winans, Harry Smith....but when we do get together it's kind of reference-room time in the Old Peoples' Home.

And Moore was right in the center of things.

I could always relate to him and his work. It was so close to my growing up time in Chicago during the thirties and forties, guns and gangs and all the little bars and babes and poverty and big-shot richness. I remember how, when I was in my late teens/early twenties, I'd walk around downtown on my way to a jazz club or film or play, always a babe on my arm, with one hand in my pocket, like I was carrying a gun. No one messed with me. And here's Moore's poem framed on my wall:

> reynolds thought he'd
> gotten away when he
> slipped out the back
> of maria's diner but
> montez was waiting
> near the wrecked
> buick sitting next
> to the tracks this
> almost looks like a
> scene from a b movie
> reynolds sd stalling
> montez used the automatic's barrel to
> scratch an itch on
> his cheek last words
> amigo you wanna cry
> for yr mama I have
> some money cd we
> work something out
> montez smiled it
> looked like a snake
> crawling into his
> face his pistol was
> a shadow spreading
> along gravel wind
> from the river
> brought the
> odor of shit.

Moore wanted to eliminate himself as mediator, himself as philosopher, historian, recorder. He wanted to bring you right into the reality of the reality itself.

Immediate, uncensored, un-run-around-with, no poetic personality coming in to contaminate the reality he was trying to capture. He was Mr. Reality, the most reality re-creating poet we've ever had in the alleys with a gun in his hand. The Mafia in Chicago really was in the middle of everything. The Catholic grammar school and high school I went to were full of guys who later became Mafioso. Streets, guns, sax, sex.....you wanna time-travel back to Old Chicago, just get in the old Buick named Todd Moore and gun it full-speed.

F.N. Wright
Agoura, CA

IN MEMORY OF TODD MOORE

I did not know him
personally
only through his words
words I could relate to
a poet only a few years
longer in the wooden keg
than I have been
being aged to perfection
the right taste
the words as smooth
as Tennessee sour mash
rolling off his tongue
twinkling eyes full of mischief
perhaps
or just plain ornery thoughts
dancing in his mind
but I did do a drawing
to go with one of his poems
in The Book Of Jack
just before his sudden
unexpected death
a table with a shot glass
bloodied ten dollar bill
& appropriately enough
a smoking snub-nose
.38 revolver
the smoke-filled words
leading up the stairway
to heaven from the
smoking gun.

Drawing by F. N. Wright

ALAN CATLIN
Schenectady, NY

She the devil

in a red
dress w/ a
tattoo of my
heart w/ a
dagger in it
on her arm
Kissing me
deadly,
laughing so
loud she
maybe wake
the dead

* * *

Gun Talk was

what he answered
to on the street
like some kind
of hi angel
of death w/
two hundred
dollar shades
& more gold
than Fort Knox
on his person,
a stoned fool
of a walking
target for side
alley silent killers,
blade talk

* * *

IKNEW TODD mostly through his work though we had contact through letters and e-mail periodically over last thirty years, though I wouldn't say that we were ever friends (Facebook doesn't count). I have enormous respect for his work, especially the Dillinger poems which I believe is one of the signature, truly American long poems of the last half of the 20th century. I read just about everything so that is not something I say lightly. He will be missed.

BEN SMITH
Tullamarine, Australia

Same old

Same old,
same old.

were the last
things he told me
as i hassled
him about a book
i was sending
to his spot on
san pedro.

When i asked
what he thought
about my family
ever reading my filth
he said

"i never wrote
till my old man
passed
and
i sure as shit
never wrote
for family
regardless."

i always believed
what
he said.

Todd never wrote
for no one but
the bent back
and
crooked cats
that knew writing
was too important to
have critics.

Especially the
scholars.
He said

"Dont let
sentiments get
in the way -

dont gush,
dont be sloppy,
dont waste words."

I imagine Todd,
some place
still banging em out
with his
pistol
shit

Maybe teaching
dillinger
a thing or two
about violence
and
words.

* * *

Two

I once saw a
beethoven symphony
of eroica
at the hammer hall.

The conductor
danced in his pants
and pushed his
hands to the sky
with the seeming
strength of a man
possessed.

At the moment
he stopped
and stood down,
his eyes still
wild
with the
crescendo,
i thought of todd,
and his
passing

Really just a
stranger to me,
but i thought about
his white hair
and the way he
bashed words around
the face with

a blunt
pick axe.

Stabbing words
like
Black mamba bites

or punctured lungs
letting out a
long hisssss.

If todd was a
conductor he
would use a
machete instead
of a baton

and the sound of
the orchestra
would bloat
and ebb
to the sounds
of words screaming
as he waded
across their shores
like a hungry
sea dog.

* * *

I'M NOT going to over emotionalize this. That would
be corny. I'm going to be as honest as possible. I
think that's the most respectful thing to do. I never met
Todd in person, but we kicked a few emails back forth

for a couple of years and whenever I did something I thought he might dig I mailed a copy to his joint on San Pedro St. He liked that I didn't give a fuck. He gave me my first buzz from poetry because he said I "didn't get sentimental". I was always drunk and hassling him with emails. Asking him what his family thought about his writing because it was a concern of mine. He said his dad never read any of his stuff. He was open with stuff like that; especially to a stranger. And I dug that. I'm not going to say I used that as inspiration but I sure as shit took it on board. The guy was smooth. He could run a racket. Todd was a fucking gangster. That's what I liked most about Todd. I wasn't sure how old he was but he spoke *street*. Chewed asphalt. Even through emails the cat was cool. Unrushed, controlled and then at times he gave a real "toughen up baby" attitude. His poetry is testament to that. I'd like to say he didn't pull a punch, but what would I know. I said I wanted this to be as honest as possible. If Todd read this, I could imagine him saying "the fuck is this kid blathering about". That's the interesting thing. The connection of it all. The two dudes kicking emails and chewing the fat on either end of the globe. And then he's gone, and I don't feel no different cause he was never 'round to fill up the physical space that's now empty. But mentally. Yeah, fuck yeah, filled up. And until I die; I get to keep that. The memories of his words. That's all we really shared. Words. I think it was kinda cool that way.

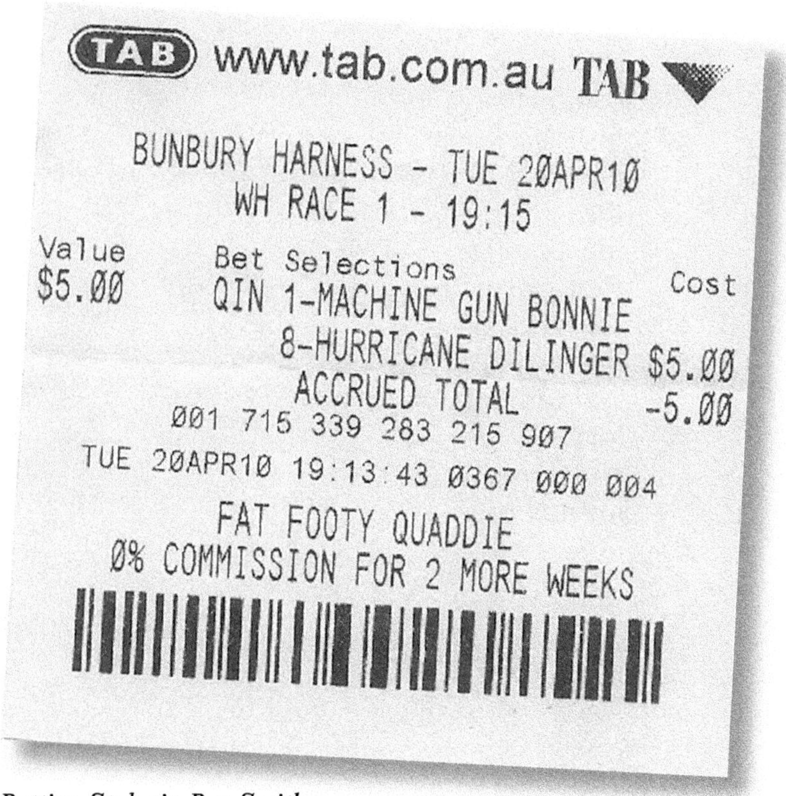

Betting Stub via Ben Smith

SCOT YOUNG
Poplar Bluff, MO

as dillinger waits

an outlaw
shot the last
colt forty
five *ricochet*
ing through
the universe
like tequila
shot glasses
slammed on a
sawdust floor
and tonight
lola
will dance
for no one

GARY BROWER
Placitas, NM

DILLINGER'S BIO

graphy
ended
at the
Biograph
The
ater
am
bushed
by the FBI
after a tip
from Billie's friend
till (decades later)
an outlaw poet
pumped words
into Dill
inger's
remains
&
Public
Enemy No. 1
of the bankers
& J. Edgar
flickered
into action
again
in the film noir
of collective

memory
a car
chase
re
su
med
sirens blaring
two black cars
racing thru
the urban night
of '34 Chicago
into the Perpetual
Present

cops
hanging
onto patrol
cars

standing on the running
boards
firing their pistols
at the Icon
in the escaping
car ahead
bullets bouncing
off the time-warp
as the death-shiny Buick
hurtled thru
the Fi
nancial
Dis
trict
the poet
as driver

of the double
Meta-Four-cylinder
getaway car as it
screeched around
corners
into the Now
when bankers
and Wall Street traitors
are trying to steal
the Nation
once again
and cops
as usual
protect the Rich
chase Robbin'
Hood
in the Infinite
Car Chase
while crooked
Pols
bank on Big Money
from our legalized
corruption
but
when the Rich
get away
with stealing
from the Poor
in the continual
Class War
outlaws
will come out

of the woodwork
to balance

the banker's
checkbooks
till
Che
comes
along.

* * *

NIGHT-CLERK AT THE DILLINGER HOTEL:
A Reminiscence Of Todd Moore

I first met Todd Moore in 2005 at a party and the host recommended we get together and talk as we had a lot of interests in common. And, we did! Eventually this led to what became a pattern, we started meeting monthly for lunch at a local restaurant in Albuquerque's northeast heights not far from where Todd lived. These luncheons were more than lunch (they generally lasted around 3-4 hours), we talked about poetry and literature in all genres, locally, nationally, internationally. Todd was very well read in world literature and we would discuss authors from Orhan Pamuk to Cesar Vallejo, from Lorca to Pasternak, from Cavafy to Neruda, The Beats to the Black Mountain Poets, not to mention the local poetry scene. We met for these luncheons for the last few years. A couple of times Tony Mares, one of New Mexico's most well known poets, dropped in too. We might discuss the role of the poet in Nobelist Orhan Pamuk's novel Snow as compared to the same in Pasternak's Doctor Zhivago, or maybe the latest new edition of Cavafy's complete works, or a new book out on Mayakovsky and his work, or Rita Dove's book Sonata Mulattica, poems about the unusual story of a mulatto boy who became a classical violinist, playing with Beethoven, and the tragic ending.

Todd, Tony Mares and I had a poetry reading together a few years ago at Airdance Artspace in Albuquerque's South Valley which drew a big crowd. Todd also had read at the Duende Poetry Series in Placitas, once with Mark Weber and the Bayou Seco musical group, and once with John Macker and I in a segment of the "Placitas Literary Traditions" reading of a few years back, presenting the poetry of Ed Dorn. The poetry of Creeley and others were also presented at this reading by some 8-10 poets. (Todd, Macker and I are/were all fans of Dorn's poetry).

Ed Dorn lived for a short while in Placitas, having followed Robert Creeley there. Creeley lived twice in the village, which was and is, to some extent, still a sort of artist's colony since today an approximate 25% of the populace of this unincorporated village (which has its own wild horse herd) are artists of one kind or another, not to mention the beautiful views from the foothills of the 10,500-foot Sandia Mountains which the village abuts. Although a known poet, Creeley came to the University of New Mexico to study (he received an MFA) and then to teach, and lived in the village. Placitas was also known in those days for its four hippie communes, the poetry readings at the local Thunderbird Bar and the many artists who lived there. In addition to reading, Todd attended many of the poetry readings in the Duende Poetry Series of Placitas just as a member of the audience. The Series, now in its seventh year, is always held at the local winery.

Todd also participated in the April Poetry Month events in Albuquerque organized by Dale Harris, editor of the poetry magazine Central Avenue for the five years of its existence. And, he read from time to time at the Winnings Coffee House readings that were organized in tandem with Central Avenue. He also read in the poetry series at Acequia Booksellers and at various other readings in Albuquerque. Todd was, in other words, well integrated into the New Mexico poetry scene, and was seen as one of the elders of that community. When he arrived in the Albuquerque area, after retiring from his teaching position of many years in Illinois, he published a book of poems to announce his presence in the state and to say hello to the poets who live here, it's called Working on my Duende. In it, he names many of the well known poets of New Mexico, to say he was here, to let them know he knew of them and knew their work. He also, over the years, integrated a lot of New Mexico imagery and stories into his poetry, even in Dillinger, where he has Dillinger driving through New Mexico and meeting a local Native American who is also a poet and artist in the traditional sense.

We miss his physical presence though we still have his poetic presence here in his adopted home, among the beauties of the Sandias, Bosque del Apache, cholla, chamisa and the malpais*.

If he were the night clerk in a local establishment called The Dillinger Hotel, he would look out the window and say: "The Badlands are everywhere." And that's why we have poetry and all kinds of art in every corner of the state. You can be inspired by the nature, cultures and history here, you can create something good in the malpais of the Land of Enchantment.

Literally bad (mal) country (pais).

JOE SPEER
*Heaven**

TODD MOORE

WHENEVER we pass through Albuquerque, NM I call Todd to arrange a meeting at the Frontier Restaurant. He always arrives first and secures a booth near the front door. This business end is constantly busy and to find the same seat every time at a random hour is a gamble. How does he do it? My guess is that when Todd swings through the glass door the occupants of said booth automatically vacate or maybe the management reassigns them another place in the back room so Todd commands the best view and easy exit.

We look into each others' eyes for what seems to be as brief a time as squinting at a target, but actually two or three hours pass. He makes several trips outside to put more coins in the parking meter. Talking with Todd about literature is invigorating. He suggests ways to improve or raise the ante on our distribution. Todd knows we travel extensively and he recommends we create a regional calendar of open mics. As a result our Beatlick News includes venues from Oaxaca to Berkeley.

It amazes me how quickly he can write a poem. I go to the counter for a coffee refill and when I return he has a complete poem to read me. Todd can write a poem like

---

Regrettably, Joe Speer passed away in January of this year, from Pancreatic Cancer. It was swift and unexpected. So, chances are, he's shooting the shit with Todd somewhere out there on another plane of existence…so long Joe, it's been good to know you…

he is dealing cards. His pen moves even while looking at you. We usually exchange material and I put the touch on him for a piece to use in our publication. I leave our interview elated and stimulated and not in the mood for the flat humdrum look of Central Avenue. I cross to the university and walk to the Fine Arts Library to watch a movie, maybe a film noir that Todd saw years ago. I believe we will hear more from Todd.

The next time I visit the Frontier I will not be surprised to see Todd at the same booth, having a chat with John Dillinger. John has a violin case next to him and Todd is packing a stack of chapbooks and a CD.

GARY GOUDE
Riverside, CA

FIRE RAIN
For Bill Shields

We exist only to suffer
and the gods are watching
for any sign of bravery
and there are few.
Those who endure
must shine and burn
for the rest to see.
I am looking at those names
on that black granite slab, Bill
and I can see
forever.

*Previously published in Looking with Bleeding
Eyes for the Tiger (Vae Victis Press)*

* * *

JOHN DILLINGER'S GHOST

THE FIRST time I read anything by Todd Moore was
sometime in 1990. I came across a few of his poems
in Wormwood Review. I was immediately struck by the
hard stark punch and deadly precision of his style. I don't
recall the poem titles but I do remember that I knew right
then that this guy was writing a kind of poetry that was
at once riveting and scary because of the way he could
lay down a line that was bone chilling simply because of
the visual imagery he invoked. I also saw that he did this

without wasting a single word. Moore used his typewriter like Dillinger used his Thompson. The words were deadly bullets, each word a bullet. So, I began to look around for more of his writing. It didn't take long to find more of his poetry because I soon discovered that Todd Moore was one of the most prolific poets writing at that time, and his style is unique, is impossible to duplicate. I ordered his two Dillinger books that were available from Primal Publishing. These two volumes are only part of Moore's epic long poem, Dillinger. I believe Todd achieved in this incredibly large poem something akin to the Great American Novel but in a poetic genre that he invented. Again, it is at once the longest poem perhaps ever written by an American poet, and without a doubt takes brevity to a whole new level with the economy of words and precision of lines that grab you and hold you to the page.

I began a correspondence with Todd Moore around that time that lasted until his death last year. He was always very generous with his advice to me about my own writing, and I consider him a mentor as well as a friend. Todd Moore is in a class all by himself as a poet. There are only a handful of poets that I consider achieved a truly unique style and managed to master the art form in their lifetime. Bukowski is one such poet. Todd Moore is another. I was very saddened to learn of his death, yet at the same time I know he achieved an absolute mastery over his own style and I suspect he sensed this prior to his passing. Besides being among the very few poets who I believe belong in the cannon of outlaw writers, Todd Moore was my friend, and I miss him.

HARRY CALHOUN
Raleigh, NC

Groin death
(for the short-and-savage-line school of poetry)

sal sd look
here my willy's
limp as a homo's
wrist but then spit
a hawker and sd
so what I'm a
man I've handled
worse like ar
bitrary line
breaks no biggie I
'll just rip
off the dick
of the first
guy who crosses
me and sew it
to me w/monofilament
line & I sd
but sal what
am I s'posed
to realize about
life from this
poem and he sd
I don't care
faggot I write
real man poems
& if you don't
like it you
better cover

yr crotch & I
shut up &
felt my balls
crawl up inside
me like landing
gear guarding against
groin larceny
& thought so
that's poetry

Originally printed in Chiron Review
Volume VII, No. 1

* * *

This is a parody of the "short-and-savage-line" school of poetry in general and Todd Moore's stuff in particular. For what it's worth, here's my two cents' worth on Todd Moore. It will not likely make me very popular in poetry circles, but here goes:

I found Moore to be derivative and prolific, not necessarily a good combination. Lyn Lifshin is also prolific, but I do remember some of her individual poems. Not so with Moore's. As a poetry editor in the '80s, I saw a ton of writers trying to do what Moore did. Basically, he was out to shock, so he had a lot of raw imagery. And the short lines, and the use of abbreviations (sd, wld, &, and so on) and the overall posturing just struck me as the opposite of what Moore was trying to accomplish. He was trying to come across as a hardass, but he came across to me as the diametrical opposite: cutesy. To me, Ron Androla wrote in Moore's hardass style with more raw energy and vigor than Moore ever did — and Androla had a softer, lyrical side, something I never saw Moore exhibit.

I'm never happy when one of our ranks shuffles off to that great slam in the sky, but I think I'm one of the few who really didn't see anything particularly special about Moore's work. And of course I could be wrong about him. But having read *The Gunfighter Elegies,* one of his last works, I don't think so. If writing in short lines with a lot of macho posturing makes you an "outlaw poet," then by gosh I'll bet I could be one too.

However, whatever I think of Todd's poetry, one thing is sure: the man deserves a tribute such as you are doing. I would hope that when the vultures eventually come for my liver that somebody would find me fit for such treatment. If not, then maybe Todd's heavenly spirit can cackle from the rafters and say, "Calhoun, you dumbass, you finally got yours." But somehow I doubt it. I might not have been his biggest fan, but he was a good guy and a straight shooter. And that's damn hard to find, these days or any time.

DAVID S. POINTER
Somewhere, USA

Off Base

the
gas-station
stomp down
was good
until Roy and
Ben told
the Marine
they were
going to use
him as their
battleship
bitch then
the Marine
picked up
the darkness
like a tire
iron and
turned them
into curb
remnants
to be read
in a lab

(previously published at St. Vitus Press)

* * *

Spotter Scope

one fully autocratic government issued
tissue disposal unit
                    watches

another become the first recon ranger
this month to ride out of a new marriage
on a Budweiser horse drawn chariot

splashing in free range fantasy sips
with sand, rock pocks-the snarl of

                    history

Miles J. Bell
UK

The poet as superhero
(for Todd Moore)

special abilities:
to step out of the
whirling idiot dance
over the perimeter
and watch from the edge
for a second
to find words in the air
like blossom or
vampire bats
nail or slide them
onto the page
making something
out of anything & nothing
maybe make
that old dance
a little easier
somehow

these superheroes
don't wield lightning bolts
fire shuriken from their fingertips
or wear capes
at least not in public
they don't leap or collapse
tall buildings
or trap bad guys
in the web of justice
they can't hurl buses
                    but sometimes they can fly

Todd Moore & Miles J. Bell, London 2006

PATRICIA WELLINGHAM-JONES
Tehama, CA

Play me

Play me the song of Earth,
the one that starts with the hiss of rain,
drum rumbles of thunder
and the underground thrum of bass.
Play me the stars that throw
shaft of night light and a moon
that swirls the seas.
Play me the lava that bubbles
and seethes below then
screams toward air.
Play me the song of life,
its haunting melodies,
strange variations.
Yes, do, play me the song of Earth.

Todd at work, Walnut Creek, CA 2009. Photo by Barbara Moore

BELINDA SUBRAMAN

*Left to right: Mark Weber, Judson Crews, Belinda Subraman,
Todd Moore, Wendall Anderson, Ramanth Subramanian*

THE PHOTO was taken at Judson Crews' apartment in Albuquerque, NM. Ram and I used to go see Judson two or three times a year. At some point Mark and then Todd moved to Albuquerque too and it was great for a bunch of small press poets to meet and yammer. I think we all considered Todd the "star" of the group. He had a cult following even years ago. I reviewed his Dillinger books in *Gypsy Literary Magazine* and he signed one to me personally in Albuquerque.

Todd's brilliant story telling of violence, blood and lust surely was a deep part of him but you'd never guess such writing could come from a mild mannered middle aged school teacher. He seemed humble, gentle, compassionate. Anything rough surfaced in his art and it pulled you in until you realized you'd read a whole book when you only meant to sample a few poems. He was simply brilliant.

DALE HARRIS
ABQ, NM

Todd reading his wonderful "Death Song" at the Harwood Art Center in Albuquerque April 2007 in a poetry month show that I organized. He appeared with San Francisco poets Whitman McGowan & Margery Snyder and others, show was titled "White Folks Was Wild Once Too" after Whitman's signature poem by the same name. Photo by Alan Mitchell

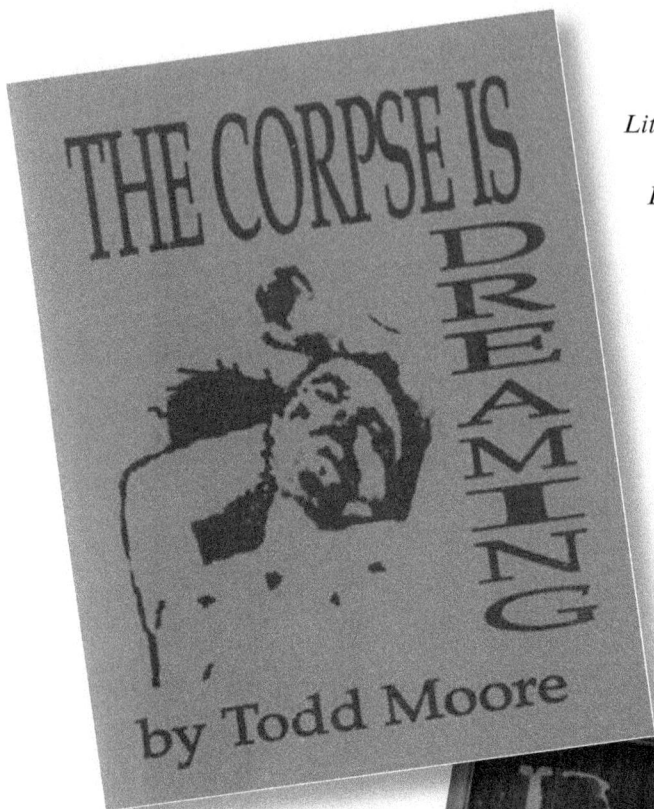

*Little Red Book #20–
one of Todd's best
Dillinger sections in
my humble opinion
–RD Armstrong*

*Little Red Book #4–
featuring Todd Moore
& RD Armstrong*

May 31, 2001

Raindog,

that was one helluva letter. i haven't thought much abt the caballah
for years. before i started writing poetry i'd dabbled a bit in
philosophy. that's probably where i picked some of it up. but you
are right ---- i guess i was so deeply into writing Resurrection i
wasn't aware of where some of it was coming from.

i wrote most of the poem in March & did some tightening in April.
anyway, the poem came with enormous force. i got most of it in one
sitting. it felt like getting hit by lightning. the times that
happens all i can do is sit there and sizzle. you burn from the
inside out. when i read it at the Blue Dragon i came away exhausted.
felt like a storm had blown thru me. in some ways the intensity seems
to be packed tighter.

the funny thing is i wasn't even reaching for this poem. it just
sneaked up on me. when the lines came they were irresistable. and,
they are staying that way. each time i read it to myself i feel a
tremendous surge of excitement. something kicks in i can't explain.

&, as always, it was good to hear from you --- how the poem hit you.
these things are always good to know. also, that you want to publish
it along with those other two sections.

and, i agree --- i wish there were 200 million --- i'd even take 200
thousand people who'd pay to read my stuff. 200 thousand wd be
comfortable. til then, right?

the Nick Adams stories are among my favorites. they're probably the
best that Hemingway produced. great stuff.

friends always,

Todd

<u>ABIOLA OLATUNDE</u>
Nigeria

TODD MOORE—A TRIBUTE

IT STARTED simply enough for me when I joined the MWC that is 'My Writers Circle', an online community of writers and came across John Yamrus. Initially, he didn't think much of my poetry! I wanted to learn so I asked him why he felt I was not allowing myself to unfold. He gave me an education. He invited me to read poets like Todd Moore, Locklin and Plath. He said I could learn a lot from their style, and cutting edge poetry.

The experience was for me a bit weird. I had been fed on the traditional form of poetry and this came as a culture shock. I started reading Todd regularly on Outlaw Poetry. I was stunned by his wit, his bare bones style and the black humour sometimes. I had goosebumps when I read 'coming out' or the one that had an ugly looking hunting knife in the hands of Todd. I knew what John meant.

Could I ever write like this, my reaction was sharp, definite and conclusive, No! Definitely not, I wouldn't dare, but it opened a closed door within me and allowed me to step out to see what I could do with words. It could be a hunting knife for me too. Cut through the pretensions, the frills, retain my humanity and humor as I thumb my nose at life! It was release. Thereafter I kept reading Todd. Never knew what he looked like for a while but thought he must be one hell of a man. I had never heard of the Dillinger series until John discussed it but I have held Todd in respect from reading his other poems.

Some of the poems like 'death rides the blood', 'Billie licked' were stunning, and brutally short, packed with venom in my estimation. I never could laugh reading his poems. I thought a lot about them and wondered a lot and saw the effectiveness of how he used what I called bare bones to get his points across. His supreme indifference to the trivialities of life came through to me and strangely an underlying avuncular compassion for the society.

I come from a part of the universe where our poetry is both spiritual and ritualistic and where we use words sparingly in strict conformation with our concept of the cosmos. Todd was akin to that in the use of words and on his definition of the cosmos too but he was on the side of the street I could not cross! I could thus only admire, respect and learn from him. I was thus devastated when John sent word back that he had passed.

John did give me a nodding approval later as an aspiring poet but I arrived at that point through what I learned from the likes of Todd Moore. I have this for him therefore:

Hold your knife firm Todd

To carve a seat

With the ancestors.

BRENT LEAKE
Salt Lake City, Utah

All Poets Are Outlaws

looking very much
like a retired
school teacher
that oughta be out
in the flower
garden
throwing snails
in his
neighbor's yard
he's a
freelance slinger
of poetic
utterances
poetry is language
   all poets
are outlaws
he says
placing the
barrel of his
blue steel .357
poetry maker
at your right
temple here
enjoy this one
my friend
he says
w/a hoarse
   laugh.

* * *

In Early Morning Darkness

hit men
like him
saunter
the streets
dressed
in early
morning
darkness
carrying a
cello case
full of poetry
when he's
got you in
his cross-hairs
each poem's
dead on its mark
moving at
the speed of
comprehension
you miss nothing
you understand
it all
damn near
forgetting
to breathe

* * *

THE FIRST time I met Todd Moore was on the 18th of September, 1993. The *Pearl* girls called for a poetic gathering to hail the release of Mark Weber's new collection of poetry they had just published. A bunch of us strays wandered into Long Beach, California to pay homage to Big Web and read a poem or two of our own.

It was later that evening at a house party that I met Todd. It was more of a "hey, how are ya man?" type of meeting. I was bouncing around shaking hands and saying howdy to all these folks who I'd been reading for a while, like Joan Jobe Smith and Gerald Locklin, and folks I don't even remember now.

Three years later I hooked up with Todd when I went down to Albuquerque in August of 1996 to participate in Weber's *Assembled Zen*. Mark, Todd and I had breakfast at Loyola's on Central Avenue. This joint has these breakfast burritos bigger than the entire county of Bernalillo. Taters, cheese, chorizo, avocado, sour cream and salsa...lots of salsa. Yeh, it's a serious burrito. Well, hell, it's beyond burrito, it's work of art.

Anyway, at this breakfast was the first time I was indoctrinated by Todd about his theory of poetry as language. He didn't give two hoots in hell about the academic's notion of poetic imagery, poetry to Todd was raw guttural language and that poetic language stood on its own. Ever the teacher, I learned something from Todd that I have tried to practice in my own poetry to this day.

In August of 2003, I found myself again in Albuquerque spending time with Mark Weber at his humble hacienda. Todd came over and the three of us recorded recent poems we had written. Mark and I pulled out our old guitars and laid down a couple of honky-tonk blues tracks. Todd did a little dance in his chair. We toasted each others' health, his Sprite can against my diet Dew can. We had us a damn fine time. Memories of my friend Todd I'll always treasure.

ANN MENEBROKER
Sacramento, CA

In Tribute/Are You Carrying?
for Todd Moore

I never wore a gun
or shot anyone
and other than your
poems (where there were
plenty of guns and death)
you probably didn't either.
But for all I know
you might have been a crack
shot and had bodies
under the house where
you also threw old
beer bottles and fifths of
whiskey. All I do know
is you showed up
in Sacramento at Luna's
with your wife
reading your poems
and talking about life.
All I know is the crowd
loved you and we hugged
and took pictures.
And when I think about
that visit and all our years
in this business
of poem-making
what we "carry" isn't

a .44 magnum
but the weight of a
heart and the filling
up with that corny
old word whose draw
(slow or fast)
finds its mark.

Raindog, Ann Menebroker & Todd at the Luna's Café reading in
Sacramento, CA May 09

MICHAEL ADAMS
Layfayette, CO

Do Something

Corso once said
if you gotta
rant about politics
send a letter
to the editor, & it's true there's been
a hell of a lot of dreadful
poetry written in the service of one
cause or another but I figure it's like
country music, you have to wade
through an ocean
of crap to get to Big River
or I saw the Light,

& sometimes
you get so pissed off you're gonna
explode if you don't
do something
& so at the risk of making
a big fool of yourself
you start to rant about why
can't somebody write
a poem that knocks
a few teeth out of the mouths
of all the greedheads,
the little boy
generals, the pissant
politicians,
the talkers with the stink
of death coming

from their mouths,
the Wall Street ghouls who can't wait
for us to die & grind
our bones into dog food,
& you just wish with all your
heart & soul that somebody
would write
a poem that knocks them all

On their sorry asses
& makes them whimper & beg so everybody
can see what assholes
they are & maybe throw
dead fish & dog shit at them
& get a good laugh because all that money
has got to be worth
a little blood.

* * *

Good Luck
This is my last and final will. Good luck to all of you.
Joe Hill

To all of you
down and out, broke
out on the street
out of time
out of excuses

To all of you
been pulled over, roughed up and cuffed,
wrong skin, wrong looks, wrong place,
taken for a ride

slammed in the slammer
cold, rolled and tenderized
like a side of beef

Good luck to all of you

To all of you beautiful lovers
who should have walked out the door
and kept on going but didn't and once again
bloodied, black-eyed, bone-broken,
because somewhere you learned that love
means taking it on the chin.
But good luck all the same.
And next time, keep on walking.

To the hungry and the haunted,
the hopeless and all the singers of beautiful songs
who sing to empty rooms.

Good luck to all of you.

To the needle tracked and addle brained,
who did all the wrong things
because they seemed like the only things to do,
there's always another way to go.
Take heart.
Be strong.

To the teenage mother with the skinny legs,
to the shopping cart lady on Larimer,
to all the grunts in Pharaoh's Army,
the broken and forsaken, to the legless vet
on Blake St. when the ball game lets out,
to the fury-driven soldier who can never take back
the death he has dealt.
Good luck to all of you.

To the big shorts, baggy-ass, slicked back
hip-hop gansta younger brother wanna be.
Don't go down that road.
No good ever came of messing up your brother,
and blue or red, it's not worth being dead,
don't spill the blood of another.

Good luck, but change your ways.

Good luck to all of you, brothers and sisters.
To you, sister with your two kids and two jobs
and a worthless no-good man
with the most beautiful smile in the world
who only comes around
flat broke and down and out,
or horny and hungry

Good luck to all of you
who have ever walked the line,
punched a clock, stood shoulder to shoulder,
demanding a fair shake

Good luck, good luck
To you fighters for justice, you heroes of peace
To this my land, my country 'tis of thee
Oh, sweet sweet land, where is your liberty
To the tear-gassed, the clubbed, the bloodied and the caged

Good luck to all of you
To you pickers and harp players and all you soulful singers,
goin' down the road feelin bad, to all of you who still believe
in Woody, in Leadbelly in the Blues and the Big Rock Candy Mountain

Good luck to all of you.

Good luck to all of you saintly sinners who really would
be saints if only, if only, it weren't so damn hard.

To all of you waiting for the devil at the crossroads with
your harp in your hand and that hunger greater than
the heavens that comes when you know that your arms
will never be long enough to embrace it all
Good luck, good luck to you

Good luck to all of you who refuse to fall
for the scams and flim-flam of the hollow man.

And good luck to all you lovely lovers.

Good luck to all you beautiful women,
who only grow more beautiful with each passing year.

Good luck to all you wanderers, to all of you lost dogs
who have fought your way this far and still have
a smile for your brothers and sisters
and a helping hand to lend.

We need you all.

Good luck, good luck to all of you.

E. R. Biggs
Santa Fe, NM

Initials

We carved our initials in the wind
the way William Bonney carved his own
and those of the Mexican girl too shy

to cut the sea waves that crested
against the blue-green chamisa in the hills
and the ghost wind howling in the caverns
against men with bowlers it had known
from New York City. The way

Pinkertons brought a caravan
up the valley, desert shore
with boxes tied by rope to the backs of horses
of ammunition for the Gatling guns for men
who came to him that day.

You look at me
unflinching, stern.
I grab a Bowie knife
half-dressed from the bedroom. I don't have time
for anything else.

I see the girl,
fear lighting
her eyes. I hear
the ocean roar.

The water-drowned greasewood and the yucca
dead in the sand-dry arroyo.

The last bug crawling from the noise,
its antennae waving to the breeze.

You held my knife to the wind but it made no sound.
You looked me in the eyes and did not talk.

Blood stains the floor in the cabin. Your gurgles
call back to me in a haze.

* * *

HOMAGE TO TODD MOORE

TODD MOORE made a central link in a line of poets that challenged and influenced the poetic world. Todd was unique and very different from the others, but his stylistic message was roughly the same. First, Charles Bukowski formed much of the sexual landscape of poetry in the 1960s and 70s. Then Moore, with his wild, bloody, stripped-down verse, came along. John Yamrus stalked the outskirts with his quiet, evocative minimalism. For decades they worked in the small-press shadows while much of the rest of poetry improved its image-making.

The underlying insight in the Bukowski-Moore-Yamrus line of mechanics tore at the fluffiness of much of modern poetry. Moore's prolific and critical role in this took time to sink in. Now, however, people are slowly coming to appreciate the real importance of Moore's visionary work and how it fits into contemporary poetry movements.

There's a good deal of very real, beautiful poetry out in the contemporary world. A lot of poetry in recent decades and these days, however, simply does not know itself. It can be sculpted and pretty and euphonious, like butterflies' wings in the sun, and still not mean a damn thing. This is a problem with roots as far back as the 60s, with Sergeant Pepper-style psychedelic verse. Today's incarnation of this is overwrought academic superficiality.

It doesn't have to be this way. Good writers can grab at the root of a thing, show the essence, breathe the breath of a life's meaning. But that doesn't happen by accident. It takes poets who know what they're doing. It takes knowing the basis for the real yet inferential contribution writers like Moore have made to the art. Moore's punchy, short lines on Dillinger showed the viscera ripped from his subject's surroundings. That visceral sense is what so much of contemporary poetry lacks. It's what many of us need to move to the next level. It's a hard-knocks PhD program. Without the brilliant counterweight of Moore and similar poets, we'd be adrift. The simmering brutality provided by Moore balanced the treacle of other poets. So here's to Todd Moore, a prof in wolf's clothing.

ELLIOT GORN
Providence, RI

TODD MOORE AND JOHN DILLINGER

I'M AN historian, and I recently wrote a book about John Dillinger. Early on in my research I was doing some work at the University of Chicago library. Stumbling around, looking at this and that, wondering if writing this book was such a good idea, I came across the first three volumes of Todd Moore's Dillinger saga.

I was transfixed. I knew that I could never do what Moore did. Historians' work, of course, is more prosaic, in every sense of that word. Getting the story fully and accurately is useful enough, but Moore had a poet's gift for language and imagery, a powerful sense of the mythic, and the guts to express it all. His Dillinger poems gave me confidence that I was onto something, that the Dillinger story was elemental, richly American, and well-worth trying to understand.

My last chapter is about how the Dillinger legend refuses to die, and how artists like Moore keep finding something new and compelling about the story. Shortly after my book came out last summer, Moore was kind enough to write me a note about it, and we exchanged a few letters. He couldn't have been more gracious, and I was flattered that he'd noticed *Dillinger's Wild Ride*.

In an essay titled "The Dillinger Convergence," published shortly before his death, Moore said most of what anyone needed to know about the outlaw's times and ours. "When I say I have been working on Dillinger, what I really mean is that I've been exploring the life, the blood, the legend, the soul of this man as well as his complex mythology which means that I have also been exploring the dark outlaw soul of America as well."

For thirty years, Moore did more than mere excavation work; historians can handle that, that's the easy part. Moore, the poet, the visionary, made Dillinger come alive, and did so to bring america back to something we were losing. In writing the Dillinger cycle, Moore tells us, his goal was to reclaim "an america that has been shoved down into the cellar 'id' where all the social outlaws and outlaw poets have been locked away from the polite world."

Moore's life task, a mighty one, was to keep that "dark outlaw soul" alive for us, to make it real and vivid, to reveal it anew to us. Writing about Dillinger, Moore found America.

DON WINTER
South Bend, IN

FOR TODD MOORE, IN MEMORY

RARELY gathered together as a locus of critique, the elements of a sociological poetics uncover the terms and uses of most American literary "movements" as taxonomies of taste and/or group identity, joustings for a higher rung on the status ladder. The mindless, bourgeois, careerist movement of Modernism is what Todd Moore encountered when he began to write. This movement connected poetic integrity with elegance of form, was not inclusive but exclusive, self-absorbed and ignorant. Charles Bukowsi, contemporary of Moore, voiced his feeling of constriction: "I was aware of the glass prison terminology: that fancy, long, and twisted words were evasions, crutches, weaknesses." Like Bukowski, Moore did not gibber or evade; he wrung the elegance, the romance, the self-intoxication out of poetry:

> one tire
> was still
> spinning when
> larry rolled
> out it
> looked funny
> to see the
> engine on
> fire because
> steel wasn't
> supposed to
> burn & he
> almost

laughed til
he looked
back dora
was sitting
very still be
hind
the wheel w/
something
steel thru
her & the
angle of the
sun at that
time of day
made the
wind look
red

In Moore's poems such as this one, imagination and reality meet as equals. Moore, unlike the Modernists, was radically awake in his writing, with a consciousness fiercely engaged by the particularity of this world, a consciousness peddling hard as it could to attend to and honor each moment in that relentless flood of disparate sensations, experiences (and memories about sensations and experiences), and ideas which is contemporary life, and he wrote with an authority of voice rarely achieved.

One other thing. Moore knew how to make a good poem out of what seemed a forbidden voice. Craft in action. Moore's careful use of craft often becomes meaning in his poems, or underscores meaning. See what I mean in the poem above? His use of enjambment increases the speed of the poem, and the tension of the syntax. Yet a sense of restriction is also suggested by the tightly wrapped stanza. So the entangling of craft with meaning underscores not only the explosiveness of the situation, but also the idea of the character's entrapments. The poem is a sort of rhythmic oasis, enclosing a measured movement, like a dance or a march, and yet the rhythms in the poem are not metronomic. The poem has, as Haas said of great poems, a "brilliance that seems neither dictated nor wrought; it is headlong, furious, and casual."

So why haven't Moore's poems been included in the mainstream cannon of American "academic" poetry? I believe the resistance of the "academic" literary canon to Moore's poetry arises out of a failure to appreciate, or react against, the class content of that poetry, evident, among other things, in Moore's shutting out of provisional, academically vetted, bourgeois language. That there isn't a clearer concept of the "working class" is a big issue. The working class environment and real voice lack the political, social, and economic naming that might make them dynamic. And so Moore, one of the greatest poets of the last 50 years, remains an icon only in the small press.

JOE PACHINKO
"Camp Climax," CA

TODD MOORE:
GRACED WITH GUTS,
GUTTED WITH GRACE...

IT WAS at some coffee shop in Albuquerque. Seven or eight poets had read, all of them dressed in vaguely Navajo-looking clothing, or natural fiber pastels which matched the decor. They read poems about the desert, they read poems about coyotes, mesas, their dead children, corn gods, the moon, and their Latino housekeepers, and all of them made long rambling introductions full of disclaimers before reading their poems. "This next poem is about our housekeeper, Lupe, who's really been like part of the family since we became native New Mexicans after moving here from upstate New York three years and seven and a half months ago. It's about how she...." etc. It was painful and endless.

Up walked a balding guy in non-descript clothes, thick glasses, who looked like somebody's dad. He grabbed the mike and said; "If you're going to read a poem, don't introduce it. It just fucks the whole thing up." He then proceeded to read a poem full of guts and blood, violence and shadows and chunks of flying teeth. There was no reaction beyond the usual horrible limp perfunctory applause. He was speaking a language they couldn't understand. Nobody took his advice about introductions either. That was Todd Moore.

> *i saw*
> *the black*

jack coming
ducked &
shorty took
it full
in the
face blood
& snot
flying out
of both
nostrils &
he went
sideways
howling
& a
tooth in
the air
went
w/him

He was not an academic. He never bought into the notion that poets are some superior airy fairy elite; "The poets want peace! The poets know things ordinary people don't know! The poets will save the world with their poems! The poets practice senseless acts of aromatherapy and seek the bright elusive butterfly of love, and all their pathetic drama, all their obnoxious egotism is justified because we NEED them." This goes hand in hand with the academic corollary that poetry should not be easily understood. In fact, if NOBODY understands it, including the poet, so much the better. Not so with Todd. His writing is clear, concise, and charged with his contempt for the bloodless, the gutless, and the precious.

He cherished the authentic. He was also a craftsman. In Todd's poems you see exactly what he wants you to see, you can watch them like movies. And you feel the constant implied menace of dark forces just beyond the edges of the action. As well as the mystery of what happened before the action in the poem, and what would happen after it. When he wrote about himself, he was always just another figure in the landscape. The focus is always on the story. He was tough, he never gave up. Many "Poets" disliked his work, not because they didn't understand it, but because, I believe, they understood it too well. He made them look bad. He made them and their work look boring. His work now stands as the best example I know of, bar none, that poetry is not just a bunch of namby-pamby bullshit. His work reminds me to focus on truth, on the visual, the real, to punch life into the words. To spit blood on the page and keep a loaded gun next to the typewriter. And I owe the bastard a drink. Now I'm going to have to die to buy it for him. Goodbye Todd.

A promotional flier put together by Raindog at Lummox Press for Todd's Dillinger section, The Wolf in the Cornfield...

RD ARMSTRONG
Long Beach, CA

> The gutsy writer
> Has a hernia
> The irony is golden
> Old age has nearly
> Disemboweled him
> And still he can't
> Be stopped
> His words
> With sniper-like
> Accuracy can hit
> A target from
> Three hundred yards out

* * *

*Todd & Raindog in John Macker's kitchen, Las Vegas, NM 2006
Photo by S.A. Griffin*

LETTER TO A FRIEND IN ALBUQUERQUE

Todd; I was listening to your poem
About Tornado Jones on that CD
Mark sent me and when you talked
About the music calling to him
Especially when the moon was rising
And the wind was in the trees
I *knew* exactly what you meant
I too have felt it, *tasted* it, even *smelled* it
Even though the moon I see rising
And the sound of the wind in the trees
That I hear is only in my imagination
Because when I look out my window
What *I* see through the bars…
There's no moon
No trees
And no wind
Only the dusty brown sky
Or if it's late
The shapeless steel blue of
An urban California night
Silence punctured by
The slamming of doors
The siren's wail
And the laughter of someone else's woman.

JOHN DORSEY
Toledo, OH

second hand unicorns
for Todd Moore

here sirens chime like church bells in a tombstone factory
and i think of you
how you will never
get to shoot at dragons
with a tommy gun on the streets of laredo

how lorca came back
as a firefly his wings dipped in blood

how there is never enough time for anything

how we seem to
live our lives in dog years

when it is my time
i want to be reborn
as a second hand unicorn

i want to be
a citizen of oz again
clicking my heels
together in a arizona dust storm

i want to be
a fly on all
of the walls in heaven

a tumbleweed on the
very last breath of the dead

i want to come back
on the lips of dreamers
on the mouths of young lovers

i want to believe
that all being an outlaw
really means is having
the ability to love

i want to wake up dreaming
a tune i can't remember the words to
your last poem tucked inside
my heart like a bullet

like a secret
that will only
come out in song

John Dorsey & Todd Moore, Super Chief Reading,
Las Vegas, NM 2006. Photo by S.A. Griffin

Nelson Gary
Los Angeles, CA

TODOS

I.

ICOMMUNICATED with S.A. Griffin, who recently blurbed my *Twin Volumes*. Our writing lives have crossed paths again, meeting as requested to contribute to this book. We shared mostly about how death and dying have entered our every waking moment as of late because of the condition of loved ones in our lives, having nothing to do with the death of the poet Todd Moore, which happened the day I finished the advance review copy of *Twin Volumes (TV)*. He was the first person I called to read *Twin Volumes*, only to discover he had died, so it never happened. We communicated while I was in the process of writing *TV*, and I am keeping this essay as a process instead of a product, so that maybe others can communicate with Todd's shade. I do not tempt to court the occult in speculating about his death and the completion of *TV* happening at the same time being a sign. There is nothing to think about on a gut level. It is a sign, says the viscera. Of what I do not know, but that is where faith beats knowledge every time. Faith is unlimited whereas knowledge is limited; may poetry never stop reminding us of that—like Moore's *Working on My Duende* does. It shall continue to do so for a long, long time. Todd's title gives **duende** the resonance of karma as it truly does possess, and this should be known by everyone.

Lorca's belief was that death cast the best shadow in which to write. In my experience with **duende**, the spirit behind flamenco dancing, bullfighting, and death, this is untrue. When death takes someone close and puts another person on a deathbed and another on life support, it is closer to a total eclipse of the sun during forced limbo for the living, whose awareness becomes warped, *liminal*, though everyday concerns still need to be addressed, and a *bardo* or kind of Lurianic transmigration takes place with the dead and dying as guides—oddly enough. It is good to write about what you know, and in order to know this experience, you cannot be writing and trying to edit by rereading in the dark while it is going on; this is hiding and shameful cowardice. Lorca was on to something, but he did not quite know when to stop being an aspect of *himself*, a poet, and be a human being.

All human beings die. Great works live on no matter who does them. Immortality is a cushion in the shape of a book.

It is a cushion to fall back on during trying times when one's own wisdom is hardest to access. Turn, turn, turn to access part of humanity's dowry, inheritance, regardless of humanity's shape. Todd Moore is known as an outlaw poet. Ovid, who was exiled, was an outlaw poet. When I think of an outlaw writer, I first think of Jean Genet, then every other writer and poet who has been censored or outright banned or edited unto dilution. I never think of Todd Moore as an outlaw person of letters. He was a librarian and an English teacher, but he did write about an outlaw in a way that did not conform to conventional standards, so I see his work as being outlaw poetry, even the work of his that is not about John Dillinger, and ultimately, what is against the grain of its time is for the ivory tower of tomorrow. I don't know if Todd's work deserves to be taught in universities around the world and preserved, kept vital, or not. There is a difference between an outlaw poet and outlaw poetry; or is there? I am not a critic number one; number two, I am too busy with death.

I have some other concerns.

Todd wrote an inordinate amount about death, though thankfully most of humankind never knows the nature of death about which Todd wrote—violent, violent death. As every single serious writer-poet does, who has "a life" outside the austere solitude of study and letters, Todd had the conviction that what he had to write was important. It was so important that it took him away from people, places, and things he loved far more than the written word.

It is understandable for a writer to want her or his work to be read after she or he dies. It is commitment there in the words wherein they spent most of their time and energy—to the logos behind the words. Because of this, for instance, when I read Shakespeare, my consciousness meets his in so much as what was most quintessential to him about the human experience is there for me to read in my personal experience. Yes. Any writer who writes well lives on in their work. Yes. Writing is the closest, most minimal tangible condensation of a human being's senses and intellect, even bodily self, and though the writer may be dead physically, the writer energetically is quite alive, when read. Yes.

The words are where the writer-poet has placed most or all of her or his energy. The reader catalyzes that energy and metabolizes it through the eyes, heart, gut, and mind to the point where he or she (the twin, as Baudelaire interpreted the reader) lives with the writer. The reader is as flux that vitality calms, but not to a static point. The solidity of the words apparently written on the page is actually chiseled in marble in the metaphysical sense, the real sense given that the author is dead and the reader is quite alive.

It does not take a critic to discern whether or not the work of Todd Moore will live on; it takes someone with a little common sense. Here, we are, definitely S.A. [Griffin], writing about a dead man's work, and it is alive, oh yeah! Interpreting its impact on me is a sensation similar to dream/nightmare. I adopt this reality as a stylistic intention to keep intact here in this essay and give to readers—night terrors.

I remember the night terrors I suffered the night before my beloved father-in-law passed away and my mother ended up on life support in ICU. In the nightmare section of the terrors, I was indoors, the front entrance of my home, and there was the grim reaper, not Lady Death (and certainly not Helen Aja Hammersmith-Bond, my *maggid* and the main character in *Twin Volumes,* who terrified Todd to no end). The grim reaper (who has no symbolic value to me in comparison, to say, something that does, such as a cross) knocked my head clean off my neck. Quickly my skin rotted away from my skull, but I was still conscious. All of this seemed as real as me writing this now. The grim reaper screamed at me, "Death is not love!" I screamed, eyes open in bed, unable to shake the phantasmagoria of the nightmare. I closed my eyes and saw only an electrical storm. I opened my eyes, and the darkness was carved by lightning bolts slashing the darkness not to death, but to gruesome disfigurements of charred remains. I finally was able to get these visions, night terrors, out of the forefront, but I was frightened to go the kitchen and get some milk or something, for in order to do that I had to pass the front door. And although all rationality knew there was no grim reaper there and that, of course, we are all born with the void, the emptiness, which we try to fill with everything other than what it is; because it is too unthinkable that the truth is we are incomplete, not whole people, without our deaths taking place...mmhmm. Well yes, this is the void within us, then without for the rest of the world's exhibit, and although I know there is no birth-growing-decaying-death, life-cycle jack wagon, and only the first law of thermodynamics (energy can neither be created nor destroyed, therefore, no narrative, kids, no beginning, no end) and that Todd Moore lives through another language more solid than the alphabet, though less eternal on the material plane—the language of DNA—through his children, I was scared to get out of bed and make a move for that cold refrigerator and whatever there was within that was far colder than I was in the heat of that dreadful night.

I'm very old school, and Todd, thank God, really respected that about me. It was easy for him. He was the same way.

Nevertheless, I do want to do right by Todd. I liked Todd rather a lot as a human being, and as a poet, I really thought he had the right stuff. I wouldn't have called him first thing after finishing the advance review copy version of *Twin Volumes* had I not. I used to call him Todos ("everything" in Spanish). Of course, I never called him that to his face, and I never called him that behind his back—to others as kind of a laugh or a potential windup should I be in a bit of mischievous mood.

I have no trouble writing a meaningful piece on Todos (though I would do so, even if I did not think his work was deserving, for he did place himself in that tomb of a study for so long), because I know how that solitude can crack into alienation and the whip can shred the psyche into confetti cast out a window, and all on this note has been stated rather completely—as of now and here.

II.

In *Working on My Duende*, Todd Moore gives the reader the most obvious, basic, upfront statement about the nature of how Eros and Thanatos are at one always. It is refreshingly ethical in literature for someone of his stature to do this. The following lines are the skeleton key for not only this book, but also his others, which are about Dillinger and the Lady in Red, a red as red as a wheelbarrow and as feverish and red as a rose given in passion and mourning. *Working on my Duende* shows the impulses, which collected form a spirit that informed a way of life for Todos: his own definitely and others possibly. Never more than in these lines does Todd Moore hit it harder for me as an outlaw poet through binding his personal experience with the universal embodied by *duende*. These lines are an offering of simultaneous truth and beauty that occurs because of the fusion of life and death in the plain for all people for all-time:

> *my wife barbara*
> *trims the rose bushes*
> *in our back*
> *yard the roses*
> *ring the yard like*
> *a circle of blood*
> *she takes her*
> *time snips off*
> *the proper length*
> *of growth her*
> *favorite rose is*
> *peach colored*
> *w/just a tinge*
> *of darkness at*
> *the center she*

*saves one perfect
rose for me i
can feel my
pulse shoving
darkly against
the stem working
on my duende the
same way i'd work
on a grocery list* *

III.

How did Michelangelo sculpt *David*? The great artist answers, "By removing everything that was not David," meaning his inspired vision of David. It's true what Eliot and Stravinsky say, a good artist plagiarizes, and a great one steals, to paraphrase. As a reader of books and a librarian, Todd Moore knew what I was stealing when it comes to Helen. He understood from the top to bottom, but most of all he got, at the visceral mid, the core, how outlaw that is. The idea is to steal and not get away with it, but to give people an understanding of why they need to steal this book in terms of my *Twin Volumes* being theft. Make them complicit, make them accessories. It's about motive, probable cause, yeah, PC. "And that's what the cops never understood. We were good fellas" (*Goodfellas*). Todd was scared of Helen; look at the impact Helen has already had on civilization, forming it by creating great destruction through war, which debatably was not even her fault any more than it was Homer's. Todos was wise.

This is a petition and public announcement—*bread and circuses*—to keep what was so important to the dead alive.

**This section was taken from* <u>Working on my Duende</u> *by*
Todd Moore.

<u>John Macker</u>
Las Vegas, NM

Crossing
for Todd Moore 1937-2010

He sits outside smoking, drinking & breathing
In the corpse sweet smell
Of the Aztec earth. It is pitch black,
Mexico, the hard pure universe of
Night & death

Mangas Coloradas,
   imperfect winter tool of the
gods,
astride a good pony
the rare snow last night spitballed
sideways, frosted the organ pipe,
each flake disappeared in his hand
before it could declare its
individuality, a
brittle irony
not lost on the aged chief.

Soon,
despite the hoarseness and dust furies
of
   the droughtscape,
it'll be time to harvest the macho dark
magic of the mezcal
eastern slope of the Chiricahuas.

Just north of the border,
oblivion rhymes with vermilion,

not a soul
was caught in the living act of crossing
just the winter wired coyotes;
now in his seventies,
dreams of one last score,
riding off some Fronteras rancheria's
renegade remuda
in the dark because
revenge this sweet must
be Mexican, must taste
mezcal bitter on the tongue,
the dusk glows saffron
as the earth rotates lustily
into hard shadow.

* * *

TODD MOORE, POET, 1937-2010

POET Todd Moore, Albuquerque resident outlaw, author of many books celebrating John Dillinger, passed away this morning in Tucson. He left behind two sons and lovely wife Barbara. We'd been friends for years, following our initial connection as poets. He was kind, gentle, wise, outlaw in spirit, generous, totally devoted to the word in all of its more fiery incantations. Dillinger was his chant, his channel, his obsession, his godfather, his endearing myth. He understood the poetry inherent in the dark side of Americana, of Dillinger as pop culture icon, like Bonnie & Clyde, still fascinating sorcerers in the American mainstream mind's eye.

I remember one time visiting his home and writing room filled with wall-to-wall books and the amazing collection of historic knives. The Bowie, the Spanish dagger, you could feel Todd's vibrant imagination run wild all over the blades; they were heavy in the hand like some of his books. Freighted with myth and history. His latest, maybe his best: The Riddle of The Wooden Gun (Lummox Press 2009) and Dead Reckoning (Epic Rites 2010). Small press, tough guy titles. His words, staccato machine gun bursts that fractured the American poetic line sometimes right at the joint, the syllable, are unique in American underground letters. Uncompromising lines are used as switchblades to cut into the corrupt, alcoholic gut of the American Myth. The fascinating girlfriends and gun molls of his vicious mobsters were almost as obsessed as his anti-heroes. As they seductively stroke Dillinger's lethal .38 and coo precocious bribes into his ear, they become as iconic as his gangsters.

His real life youth was full of uncertainty, violence, and adventure. He was generous as a mentor and one of the most enthusiastic and devoted practitioners of the art I'd ever met. Our first in-depth discussion, in Santa Fe, of course, had to do with Westerns, movies, books, outlaws; more Bill Holden in the Wild Bunch than John Wayne, the conversation always wound circuitously back to the poem. As he wrote in his essay, Machine Gun Dreams: "And if I had to write Dillinger at the expense of Literature, then fuck Literature. See, I wanted flesh and I wanted blood and I wanted dreams and I wanted death all mixed up in a wild desperado stew. I wanted that above all else." Amen, Todd.

Todd and I met for our last lunch together a couple of months ago in Albuquerque. He brought with him a few books he'd been reading. One was a thick book on the mythology of the contemporary frontier, another a slim volume on Mayakovsky. Another book I don't remember, but his excitement for them, for literature in general, was sincere and infectious. Absorbing Todd's love of books was like loving writing itself. He had a schoolboy's crush on outlaw literature.

I'm selling books on a slow afternoon in the gallery as I write this. An older gent, maybe about Todd's age has just purchased 2 classic first editions of the genre: Turmoil In New Mexico and Violence in Lincoln County. Two titles I know Todd had read. I swear, Todd is here in spirit, just maybe, sharing his vast knowledge of western history with the cosmos, overseeing this transaction; I know he's now out there somewhere, where Heaven is caretaker to wind-swept Boot-hills and abandoned shotgun shacks, where Dillinger has lived just as large on the edge as Todd Moore's poetry surely will.

Rest in peace, hermano.

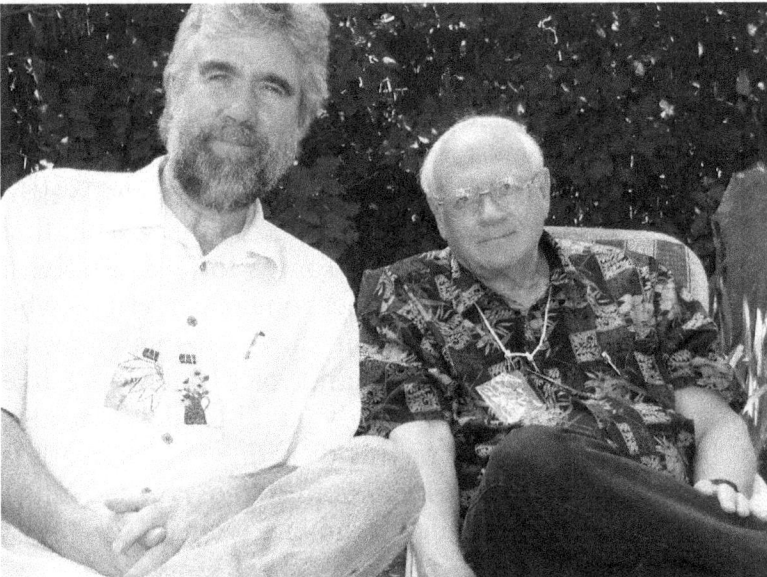

John Macker & Todd Moore

L̲awrence W̲elsh
El Paso, TX

WINGS LIKE BLOOD:
A REMEMBRANCE OF TODD MOORE

IN THE blood and wind, Todd Moore remains, and it's going to stay that way. Of course a time existed when I didn't know Moore, but that was 21 years ago. Since then, his work has remained as a guiding light of style, execution, content and language.

In poetry as in life, one should never set out to imitate or mimic another's work. The goal is to digest vast and deep quantities of poetic possibilities, and Moore was always a voice to digest. He still is, as he was in 1989. That's when I first discovered his poetry in the little magazines of the day. His cut-down style was fast, quick to the line, quick to violence and blood, and it sounded like no one else.

One instantly knew, though, that Moore had studied the masters: Robert Creeley, Zen, Cormac McCarthy, William Carlos Williams, Jack Kerouac, Lew Welch, Federico Garcia Lorca and hundreds of others, including Kell Robertson, Lyn Lifshin, Tony Moffeit and Keith Wilson. In many little magazines, one reads writers who haven't put in the time, and it shows in their lines of undeveloped language, images and voice. But Moore, like a first-rate jazz man, had already paid his dues. One also got the feeling he'd keep paying dues due to his relentless dedication to violence, which, in his hands, turned into a type of totemic, shamanic sacrament.

After months of studying his work, I knew what

I needed to do: continue to seek him out, and I found him in places like *Chiron Review, Poetry Motel, The Wormwood Review, Zen Tattoo* and many other fugitive publications. Somehow, and I don't remember how, I got his address and wrote to him. He soon replied and our correspondence started. He offered insights about Albuquerque and his new-found love for that town. I knew he hadn't lived there long, and in a sense, discovered Duke City through Mark Weber, the writer, poet, jazz aficionado and photographer.

I had discovered Albuquerque while hitchhiking across America a few years earlier, and I wanted to move to the Southwest one day, to make my escape from Los Angeles. In those days, I lived in the slums of East Hollywood, about two blocks away from Charles Bukowski's one time De Longpre address.

As I planned my next move, and my work started to appear in small magazines, Bukowski died. Moore wrote and said he would arrive in Los Angeles for a *Pearl Magazine* publication party and Charles Bukowski tribute in Long Beach. In a sense, that day served as a turning point: a chance to meet the man behind the letters and poems.

I took full advantage of the gig, buying copies of **Dillinger Vol. 1** and **2** directly from Moore, as well as a chapbook called **Chickenman,** which also contained the work of [Tony] Moffeit. During the party, Moore and Weber read, along with Southern California writers Gerald Locklin, Joan Jobe Smith and Rafael Zepeda. I had hoped to see Robert Peters, the seminal Huntington Beach poet, but that wish never materialized.

After that day, Moore promised to stay in touch, and

a few months later, I got the news that a gathering of poets, sponsored by the *Chiron Review*, would take place in Great Bend, Kansas. The meeting would celebrate the work of Tony Moffeit, but Moore would also contribute to the festivities. I made plans then to travel to Kansas.

Around that time, too, I had found a way out of Los Angeles. The University of Texas at El Paso had accepted me into its English and Creative Writing Department for a graduate degree. They offered a decent job, where I could try my hand at teaching and work on my writing at the same time. When Todd got the news, he was thrilled. For outlaws, El Paso is ground zero, and he wrote to tell me so.

"El Paso will work," he noted, and went on to talk about why it would. "Cormac McCarthy is there, the blood is there, the desert heat and smoke, as well as Billy the Kid and John Wesley Hardin..."

In some ways, his words reassured me, and I was thankful for his guidance and inspiration. When I rolled into El Paso on July 4, 1994, I knew I'd have just a few weeks to put my life together before getting on a Greyhound bus and riding to Kansas to meet Moore and Moffeit.

I think Moffeit, Mark Weber and Moore were surprised when I showed up in the tiny town of Saint John, Kansas, by myself. But there I was, fueled on the possibilities of poetry and writing, fueled on the work of Moffeit and Moore. For three days, we all hung out. Moffeit pounded his conga and read his work, and the music flowed. Moore read, Weber read and so did a gathering of others, and on the trip back to El Paso, I felt like I was a part of a circle of possibilities and kindred spirits.

And from that time on, the connections grew. When I needed to get sober, Moore wrote about his own struggles with booze and how he beat the bottle. When I was scared and doubtful, one of his letters arrived. But, of course, what counted most was the work, and he'd send new books as they came into print. In turn, I'd send him mine.

During the last five years of his life, I never knew he planned on writing about my work, but his reviews soon appeared of *Walking Backwards to Santa Fe* (Pitchfork Press, 2007) and *Skull Highway* (La Alameda Press, 2008). Not many folks completely understood what I was trying to accomplish as a poet, but Moore did.

In his letters around that time, he mentioned that a new "big" book was coming out from the Lummox Press called *The Riddle of the Wooden Gun*. He asked if I would like a review copy. Indeed, I looked forward to reading it.

In many ways, *Riddle* was a culmination of Moore's writing life, and I told him so. It was a bizarre, sprawling book where a wooden gun took the form of dream, myth, conjecture, legend, ruse, joke and miracle. It also shaped up, in my mind, as the definitive end to his Dillinger epic.

When he read the review, he was happy, and our letters continued.

Five days before Moore died, he wrote his final letter. It was a quick one, with a couple of first-rate poems attached. I was thrilled, as always, to hear from him. As usual, I filed a hard copy away in my archives, and I was working on my reply when the news arrived that he had died in Arizona.

"What's wrong, honey?" my wife asked when she

found me in our bedroom. I was walking around in tight circles and crying.

"Todd Moore has died," I said.

"I'm sorry," she said.

After awhile, I calmed down, but I was still distraught. What should I do now, I wondered? What can I do for Todd? And then the answer came: Go into the desert, light some New Mexico sage and pray and meditate. Thank the spirits for Moore's life and his poetry, and ask them to help him on his new journey, for we will all one day embark on a new journey.

On an El Paso desert mesa a few hours later, I fired up a Diamond Strike Anywhere match and lit some Oro Grande sage. I gave thanks for his life, poetry, and letters, and I knew then that a great man had crossed over, and I thought about how his work would live on, and that's when I looked up and spotted the red-tailed hawk, its wings the color of blood under the noontime sun.

I studied it, smiled and then walked away from the mesa, knowing Todd was gone but not really gone, that his spirit, like the blood, like the hawk, would always remain.

"Thank you, Todd," I mumbled and walked away.

The time had arrived then to go home, but I knew I'd never forget the vision. Like Moore, it will remain in the blood and in the wind.

MARK WEBER
ABQ, NM

BRIEF NOTES ON TODD MOORE

TODD was not only a scholar on 1930s tommygun-toting bank robbers and Wild West gun fighters, he was a psychic scholar, or rather, a psychic investigator, a deep diver into whatever might possibly be the reality of mind where such cruel, crazy, off-the-wall, blood-spattered life styles emanate.

For whatever reasons purely his own he loved going there.

Much of it had to be imaginary, certainly his own life was not that way, though he says his youth was fairly crazy.

He could come up with some strange stuff from these depths and I was just close enough of a friend that I could jump him, "Dude, are you for real?"

I never did find out what his reasonings were for spending so much time with such horrid subject matter.

At times it seemed juvenile to me, that the world surely didn't need to know about this awful stuff that it didn't need to be reminded of such things but then again, maybe it did?

Todd reveled in it, there was a sense of humor behind it all.

24may10

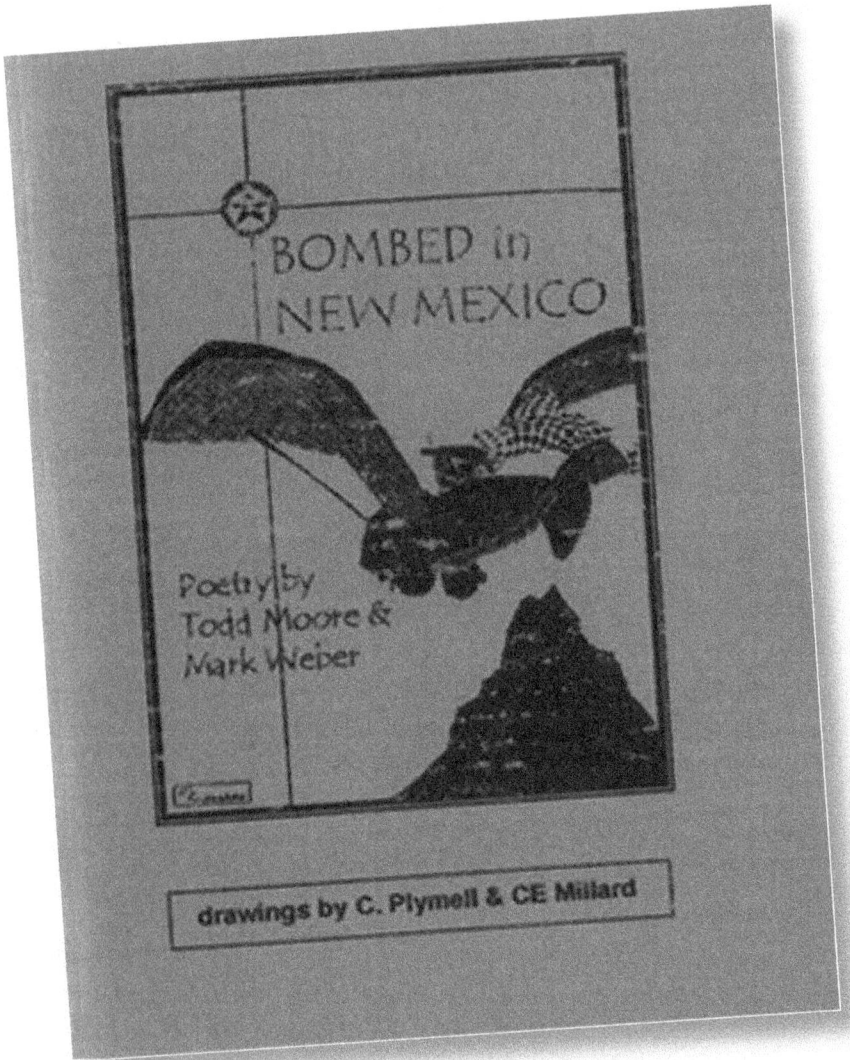

Little Red Book #26 featuring Todd Moore and Mark Weber

MISTI RAINWATER-LITES
ABQ, NM

MEETING Todd affirmed what I have always suspected...chronological age doesn't mean shit. Before getting to know Todd better through correspondence, on the basis of his poetry I assumed he was a twenty-something. Todd had more fire and magic in his spirit than men not even half his age.

* * *

I Was Poetry When Poetry Sucked Goat Balls

All the cool ass munchin' motherfuckers
were all atwitter about the latest
Facebook bonfire and MySpace swap meet.
They all wore cum beads as jewelry
dandelion wine as cologne
and me being from rural Texas
THAT'S COW PASTURE TEXAS, YA'LL
(not Austin or Houston)
of course I went to the bad place
the self-conscious in the George Strait
Jesus barbecue closet place
where it was just me and
all those Sunday school dresses
and fat rainbow markers
that smelled like licorice
and corn syrup.

I cried to Daddy
but being in Louisiana

with the redheaded BINGO hall queen
he could not hear me
for the crooked crawlin' of the crawdads
and Apostle Paul Zydeco on the radio

I cried to God
but of course that never works
George Clooney's voice
is so much more resonant
than mine
and nobody's tears are as eloquent
as Angelina Jolie's
because she is part French
also, she's a Gemini
also, she has kick ass tattoos
and knives and lipsticks
and babies and a pilot's license

God sez, "I see your Texas. I raise you
a Colorado."
I ask him about New York.
Why is it so hard for a motherfucker
to find Coca-Cola Classic in New York?
My peanuts disdain Pepsi.

Oh. And yes. I am Lucy.
Forever draped and drooling
on that cartoon piano.

But it's a hot summer night
in July and that still counts
for something in Bedford-Stuyvesant.
I've never been there
but Spike Lee

has shown me
the way.

Darling. I could cut myself
with the letters you
will never send.
I could wash down the bottle of pills
my fairy godmother gave me
with Pine-Sol
and stick flecks
of black Kiwi shoe polish
up my nostrils
because they say
the sense of hearing
is the last sense to go
but I know better
I will leave this plane
for Fantasy Island
smelling all the things
that matter most.
I will smell rubbing alcohol.
I will smell my own shit.
I will smell his Obsession cologne
because he was seventeen
and he liked me well enough
to take me for a ride
on his Indian motorcycle
and he held me beneath those stars
those Cuba Road stars in 1991
and that was the best
embrace that ever was
and will ever be.
Yes. I'm freaking out
just a little.

I'm losing track.
This is just to say I could
harm myself in various ways.
I could kill myself with a quickness.
The gas oven in the kitchen
winks at me like Rockin' Robin...
the dancer I kissed before
I left for college.
He told me he liked girls
with dark hair.
That did not stop me from
bleaching my hair myself at 22.
I've always longed for Cookie Monster blue
hair.
I've always been bothered by Cyndi Lauper's
"Time After Time" video.
The end of an affair based
on a fucking haircut?
Oh, people will end affairs
based on all kinds of inane shit.

I could walk to the wet stop
and buy some pinot noir.
I could steal stepdaddy #2's pistol.
I could make a date with the
next train.
But I
am not
cool like
that.

I'm harder than that I'm tougher than that
I'm much more cockroach la la fuckin' la
than that.

I will write tonight and tomorrow
until the poems are done with me.
The poems
will never
be done
with me.
Thus. I am poetry to infinity.
I am poetry times 666.
I'm evil in a cute Hello Kitty
kinda way.
I can scream to the stars.
I'm Cuntasaurus Rex in slo-mo.
I am fat
with mouth.

N_EAL_ W_ILGUS_
Corrales, NM

THE OUTLAW TODD MOORE

TODD Moore's works occupy a unique place in my library. Actually, it's an accordion folder containing three volumes of the Kangaroo Court DILLINGER series from the 1980s, and more recent chapbooks such as THE DEAD ZONE TRILOGY, THE SIGN OF THE GUN/RUSSIAN ROULETTE, LOVE & DEATH & TEETH IN THE BLOOD, THE RIDDLE OF THE WOODEN GUN and other titles — along with several broadsheets and pamphlets. There are also a couple of issues of Todd's SAINT VITUS'S DANCE from the days when it was still a print zine, an article on Dillinger from an old PENTHOUSE, and my 2006 interview with Todd...

The accordion folder also includes a file folder of our correspondence between 2004 and early 2010. The first few letters were between Todd's son and co-editor, Theron Moore, and I. When I expressed interest in Kell Robertson, another outlaw poet, Todd sent me a copy of his article on Kell and our correspondence began.

The exchange with Theron gradually tapered off but soon Todd and I were writing each other on a daily basis — especially when I began to review his new chapbooks as they came out. My reviews were generally positive, sometimes glowing, because I found his unique style so powerful and moving. His letters were friendly and when I sent him some of my own poems he was always complimentary. He even published a couple of my poems in SAINT VITUS'S DANCE before it went all electronic.

The ongoing correspondence led to the idea of a through-the-mail interview in early 2005, which he quickly agreed to. I had done such interviews with a number of authors back in the 1970s and '80s so it was no problem — I'd send him a batch of 5 or 6 questions and he would respond as his own schedule allowed. When I'd absorbed what he wrote I'd generate another batch for him. This process continued through October 2005 without a hitch. It was published as a chapbook a year later by Christopher Robin's Relentless Media Productions.

Even though Todd and I both lived in the Albuquerque area I only met him in person once. That was when Christopher came to town to bring the finished interview chap and Todd and others did a reading at a local coffee house. Todd, Theron and some other poets were friendly and stimulating to talk to and the get-together was a memorable one for me.

Also memorable is Todd's powerful poetry. I read a lot of contemporary poetry and much of it leaves me unmoved, bored, my mind wandering. With Todd there was no wandering. His words were so focused, so intense and moving I rarely found anything to criticize in my reviews or my own fascinated reading.

Todd Moore was one of a kind without a doubt. His poetry will surely live on for a long, long time to come. He was unique. He was an Outlaw.

* * *

INTERVIEW WITH TODD MOORE (excerpt)

NW: Getting back to **The Sign of the Gun**—*the sign is the index finger pointed, three fingers closed, thumb cocked. In sign, this hand gesture is traced back through history to mythic roots. Since reading sign i've noticed it in a number of movies and tv shows-even* **"The Simpsons."** *how pervasive is the sign? Did Dillinger and his cohorts really use the sign as depicted in your poem?*

TM: I'd like to think that the poet, like the novelist is the master inventor and therefore can reinvent history and everything it encompasses. Having said that, let's talk about the sign. According to sign theorists, no sign can ever really be symbolic. But they really haven't read very widely or they'd realize that the letter a that Hester Prynne wears in The Scarlet Letter takes on all kinds of meanings besides its original one of adulteress. Backstory: when I was a kid playing cops and robbers back in the forties and didn't have a toy gun, I'd either resort to using a broken off stick or I'd make the sign of the gun with my hand. It was a sign my father understood well and he was born in 1900, two years before Dillinger. Sometimes, when he came home and was feeling good from the booze, he'd wink, give me the sign of the gun and go bang. We both understood it as a kind of game we were all in on. It was as easily a recognizable sign to me and my friends as the fuck finger. Sometimes one of us would get brave and flash it on a cop scouting the neighborhood in a cruiser. Naturally we'd get those killer stares back. But, we all knew what it meant. I think if you're a street kid, you just simply pick up on it. Just where did it come from? That's anyone's guess. Before writing this section I spent a considerable amount of time thumbing through sign language dictionaries, books on hand signs, books on the mythologies of body signs and found very little if anything that was of any help. Finally, I came to a two part conclusion. First the sign of the gun is one of those taken for granted signals that have been around at least as long as handguns. Second, the sign of the gun is almost like a half thought out form of communication, like using the thumb for hitching a ride, using the fuck finger to put someone in his or her place, using the hand palm out to mean stop. It's simply been around so long we've taken little or no notice of it. Except when it's pointed out. As for its use among Dillinger and his gang, it probably was used but maybe with not the layered significance that I gave it. Then again, maybe it was. What I did was give the sign of the gun a history or a pseudo history. When you place a sign within historical context and then add all kinds of possibilities as to what it means in a variety of situations, then that sign becomes symbolic. As a side note, if you get a chance to see the movie Lord of War, do it. It's just a fantastic movie about guns. But, above all, be sure to watch for the sign of the gun given twice in that movie. You'll see what I'm talking about.

NW: Like you, I tend to favor narrative poetry rather than the more lyrical stuff that's sometimes hard to fathom. Do you think there's any chance poetry could make a popular comeback if it concentrated more on telling stories?

TM: I'd like to think poetry could make a popular comeback, but under the present circumstances, I don't think it will. If it does make a comeback at all, it would have to do more with the presentation rather than the content of the poem. We are a highly visual society. We're voyeur junkies. We like to watch. We have to watch. Once technology and poetry hook up and I mean really hook up, who knows what will happen. Catch this scenario: let's say you're working in some mid to above mid level bean counter position and you have five minutes to kill before you have to be in some meaningless meeting and you are carrying some kind of palm pilot or iPod gizmo that you can dial up a poet who's reading a sound byte poem and this serves as a kind of pick you up before you have to give your soul to your devil of a boss who wants that and more and you've always dreamt of becoming a poet but the work-world money's too good or you're just so addicted to a roof over your head and three hots that all you can do is dream. There are an awful lot of dreamers out there and the technology can supply that thirty second sound byte and you live right on the edge of that kind of dreaming. That could happen. The potential is there. Who knows how poetry will morph, but it will. That part of the human spirit is too tough to die.

Niall O'Sullivan
London, England

TODD MOORE IN LONDON

IT'S ABSOLUTELY fitting that Todd Moore didn't come to the attention of Londoners via some glossy supplement, or overpriced international poetry journal. I, and many others, got our first fix of Moore's outlaw poetry via the pages of a 'zine known as Rising. Still going strong and proudly dubbed "the Readers' Wives of poetry", Rising is a free publication that circulates around the most unlikely East London locations, via some deadly boozers and downmarket takeaways. Rising's Editor, the oldschool suedehead bard of N16, Tim Wells, constantly cites Moore as the inspiration to get the ball rolling and give the London literary scene something different to wine and cheese academics and the preening failed actors and rock stars of the performance scene.

While a lot of the poetry within the pages of Rising mainly concerned the lives of the protagonists, detailing many a one night stand and night on the tiles, Moore's poems stood out as a different animal, in their directness, their imagery and their purity. Unlike a lot of the other poems, I never asked myself about the person that wrote them, I just lost myself in the stark intensity that Moore built up with those short, wham-bam lines.

Jump forward a few years to 2006 and I'm running my own weekly event at Covent Garden's Poetry Cafe. I got a phone call from Wellsy telling me that Todd Moore was coming down to London and did I have space to put him on at my venue? *Todd Moore?* I replied, *ain't that the bloke*

*who does all those violent poems, the really short lines? The
Dillinger guy?* I already knew enough about Moore to give
a definite yes to Tim about the gig, but I still wanted to
know a little more. One look on Amazon showed that his
books were rarer than hen's teeth and ridiculously priced
by second hand sellers. Luckily, Wellsy came through,
handing me a couple of Todd Moore pamphlets that he
published himself and his spare copy of DILLINGER'S
THOMPSON.

I knew, Todd's "Killer Zen" poems well enough,
poems that documented those sudden explosive moments,
quick as the path of a bullet or a smashed window. But
DILLINGER'S THOMPSON was unlike anything I had
read before, consisting of the same imagery and terse,
brutal language, but stretching on and on, page after page,
a flow of imagery and narrative. No chapters. No verse
breaks. It demanded the commitment and mental stamina
of the reader even though it was almost impossible for the
reader to tear their eye from the downwards momentum
of the poem. It changed my conception of what a poem
could be.

Todd and Barbara Moore seemed no different to
your typical American tourists on the London leg of
a European vacation. Wellsy and I met up with them
at an Earl's Court hotel, and after some polite early
conversation we headed underground to get the hell
out of West London. Before heading into the station,
Todd, Wellsy and I posed in front of an anti-knife crime
poster, It featured an image of a large dagger with RIP
engraved in the handle. I remember having some kind of
altercation with some Chelsea fans on the tube journey,
which got a wry smile from Todd. The Outlaw Poet had
to make himself known at some point.

We made it to a string of East London pubs, each one a historic establishment. These were the same streets that Jack the Ripper roamed, and it was very likely that he's stopped for a beer at one of these boozers. Todd lapped it up, and the four of us happily waxed lyrical about poetry and the Outlaw way. At some point, Todd pulled out a wad of books and asked us to take our pick. I nabbed a few, including the masterful DILLINGER spoken-word album and a red-cover Kangaroo Court edition of MY NAME IS DILLINGER.

One part of NAME that always sticks in my head is the "pissing" sequence. Pissing just isn't an accepted subject for the noble art of poetry, which seeks to focus on the sacred rather than the profane. But, like a lot of Eastern philosophy, Moore's work strikes against this kind of dualism, and the power of his work comes from his ability not to make such false, dualistic distinctions. When Moore wrote his long Dillinger sequences, the world flowed through him, as the images popped up within him, they flowed out, unimpeded, onto the page. When Moore described all the places that Dillinger had pissed, he was doing what he did best, sticking our faces in the stinking reality of the world while at the same time manipulating the reader with a masterful command of metaphor. Pissing and writing are holy acts.

Speaking of which, we got through a few jars before heading to North London for Todd's first reading of the weekend. He was billed alongside Phill Jupitus (a former Ranting Poet from the eighties who had since become a stand-up comedian and national celebrity) and Hugo Williams, a well respected UK poet who had previously won the TS Eliot Prize and the Queen's Gold Medal for Poetry. Saying that Todd's reading, this one consisting of his shorter poems, split the audience would be an understatement. Half the crowd was entranced, and the other half were quite visibly repelled. This didn't seem to affect the Outlaw Poet, the poems just flowed through him as they always did. It was at the end of the reading that Todd told me that he was going to read a long poem the next day at my venue, I couldn't wait.

The gig at the Poetry Cafe was quite a different affair. A fair few members of the audience had come down from the night before, while others were UK fans of Todd Moore that had seen the gig advertised. To a hushed room, Todd read DEATH SONG, a poem about an old dying Indian by the side of a road, who fantasized about meeting John Dillinger (you can listen to the reading on this web page: **http://niallosullivan.co.uk/toddmoore-death%20song.mp3**). It was one of the highlights of my career as a live literature promoter. I've not been able to find the poem anywhere since, it might just be one of those many poems that make up the massive volume known as DILLINGER that may or may not make it into print. I still remember talking to a fan afterwards, who felt honoured to be in a room for a Todd Moore reading. He said that shivers rippled down his spine whenever Todd said the word "Dillinger".

My wife and I kept in contact with Todd and Barbara over the next couple of years (they sent us some lovely gifts including some delicious fudge blended coffee) but the correspondences became fewer as the years went on, as happens. I've always been lousy at corresponding via email, and Todd isn't the only poet whom I regret not keeping up with more frequently. It was Tim Wells who informed me in March 2010 that Todd had died. What made it even sadder was that he had just secured some funding to bring Todd over during the Summer. We all felt that Todd Moore was on the verge of breaking through on this side of the pond. The first thing I did on hearing about his passing was to make digital copies of the Dillinger CD and put them onto my mp3 player so I could once again take Todd for a stroll around London.

There was once a river that flowed through my neighbourhood, a tributary of the Thames called the River Effra. Queen Elizabeth once sailed down it in order to meet Walter Raleigh. The river was diverted underground with the building of the city's sewer system. You can still see it existing as the odd trickle here and there. That's how I think of Todd's work, there was a great river of energy that flowed through him and became manifest in his poetry. Dillinger was the key figure that summoned it up. Now that Todd Moore is no longer with us, the river has returned underground, into the dark of the unconscious. It returns every now and again in little trickles as the rest of us catch the magic every now and again, but it will take no less than another giant such as Todd Moore to summon the river into full view.

Tim Wells, Todd Moore and Naill O'Sullivan in London, 2006

FATHER LUKE
Portland, OR

one good poem

I have as much room for heroes as your average
truck driver has for poetry. There's work to be
done, bubba, and I can't be dicking around with
poesy.

Todd Moore said he wanted to write one good
poem. One poem without anything extra. He'd
read my stuff, and commented on my writing. I
won't tell you what he said, because it's personal
to me, but I liked it.

I never thanked him for that. Not to his face.
I read him. You want to give an author a gift?
Read them. When you read someone, you come
away with your own experience. Todd Moore
read me. I've read him. I still read him. It's the
maximum exchange of love possible between
authors.

Todd's dead, and you can't reach him. He can
still reach you, though. Read him. He'll touch
you with one good poem.

CASEY QUINN
Charlotte, NC

a bullet is a gift

there is security
in this roof
in this crappy nine to five
in this used Toyota
in this home cooked meal
which is taken for granted

but who knows affection
unless now and then
a bullet ricochets
from a block away
and crash-lands
through the front window
fired while two assholes
fight over nothing

* * *

an appetite for death

i think the nursery rhyme
had it right the whole time

from birth we leave a trail
of breadcrumbs back
in hopes of returning
to where we started

but in the real world
the bird doesn't eat our path

death does
to ensure we follow
the white pigeon forward

this way
only he knows the path back

* * *

shadow boxing

man vs the unknown
in the hallway
of a poorly lit home

punches thrown at nothing
tires the arms without making
a dent in the opponent

he knew more about
the subjects of life and death
when practice was over

The typer was found out behind John Macker's house in
Las Vegas, NM in 2006. It was near Tony Scibella's Shrine.
Photo by Raindog

S.A. GRIFFIN
Los Angeles, CA

THE POEM IS: TODD MOORE, GODFATHER OF OUTLAW POETRY

FOR SOME years Todd and I had been appearing in the same small press mags and zines. However, it wasn't until I took up the editorial task of The Outlaw Bible of American Poetry that we really connected.

Todd's stack of poems submitted for the book were stunning. It was all the convincing that I needed, without question, he was in and he was going to have his own section in the book. Todd figured I might take one or two, maybe three; I took them all. Working with Todd was one of the true editorial highlights for me during the course of the project, marking the beginning of a new friendship that would continue for the next dozen years, Todd and I keeping in touch primarily via email and phone calls.

I flew out to Albuquerque and Santa Fe a few times to read with Todd and to spend time with him, the last being Venus In The Badlands in April 2006. I always had a fantastic time with Todd. We'd stay up late and long into the night talking and laughing, going on about writing, poetry, family and politics. Recurring themes included Charles Bukowski, Cormac McCarthy, Jim Thompson, Sam Peckinpah, Bowie knives and of course, Dillinger. We talked about those among us we admired as fellow poets and writers, the up and coming itchy young guns that had the flaming gift. The venerable old timers gifted with the fine madness of the muse.

I was lucky enough to see Todd and his wonderful wife Barbara in May of 2009 when I went to hear him read at Book Soup on the Sunset Strip. It was Todd's tour with Raindog celebrating the Lummox Press release of The Riddle of The Wooden Gun; a great reading, Raindog and Todd splitting the bill. Predictably sad to say it wasn't much of a crowd, but not many come out for poetry on a Saturday night along the snaking electric wilderness of the Sunset Strip, parking's a bitch and then some. It would turn out to be The Moore's first and only visit to Tinsel Town. After the show we had little time, Todd and Barb wanted to see the Hollywood of legend, so we shot over to Barney's Beanery for grub and conversation.

Talked to Todd in late February of this year, calling to solicit material for my Poetry Bomb project, and to ask if I could stay with he and Barb while I was in Albuquerque during the course of my couch surfing tour. Everything was a go, poems in the mail. I would never have the pleasure of speaking with my friend again.

I got the sad and shocking news that Todd had stolen away into the moonlight quite suddenly on March 12, 2010. The Godfather of Outlaw Poetry meets the King of the Beats in golden eternity, Neal at the wheel, a patient Dillinger grinning at the pearly gates, beloved Billie by his side.

Here, inside the dream factory it is much the same as it must be anywhere else; the sun comes up, the sun goes down. Hearts are made and promises are broken inside the simultaneous orgasm of the sun as it illumes what seems to be a flat world. It is now mid September as I write this on the heels of a stillborn summer. It has been a tumultuous year rife with grieving and loss as we carry on into a new and elevated season of fear, the poem invincible inside the crucible of change.

I would take all bets that in time, Todd's Dillinger opus, will be held up as one the greatest poetic works of post WWII America.

Thanks for everything amigo, I will never forget the laughter.

* * *

The following is lifted from an hour-long interview conducted with Todd Moore on my blog talk radio show **Onword,** *May 30, 2007. On board were myself, co-host Stacey Mangiaracina, our guest Todd Moore and call-in guest Scott Wannberg.*

S.A.: How many words do you think you've channeled vis a vis John Dillinger? What, like three quarters of a million at this point?

Todd and S.A. both start laughing over the question...

Todd: Conservatively probably a quarter of a million, yeah. If it ever comes down to being between covers, it might take some serious editing, but it's probably gonna be between fifteen hundred and two thousand pages.

S.A.: Wow.

Todd: Right in that zone.

S.A.: Well, I do look forward to the day that you will have everything in one volume. Is that going to happen someday? Is it possible? Do you have everything together?

Todd: Yeah, I've got it all. I've gotta do some editing, but I've got it all here. I've got it saved. Some of it's on floppies, and some of it I've got to download, or print up.

S.A.: Do you have a favorite section of the book? Is there something that you feel especially close to?

Todd: There's a couple, there's probably three or four... talk about sections, there're probably about a hundred sections of Dillinger.

S.A.: Jesus Christ, I'm way behind man. I've got about maybe ten sections.

Todd: It's about a hundred sections, and each one is about a thousand lines or more. Ya know, somewhere in that zone. But I like The Name Is Dillinger, that was the first one I ever did back in '76, didn't get published until 1980. About two or three years ago I wrote The Dead Zone Trilogy.

S.A.: Yeah, that's great.

Todd: That's the real, solid ending of Dillinger.

S.A.: John Dorsey and I reviewed that for you, right?

Todd: Yeah, you did. Actually, thank you very much, a belated thank you, that was a tremendous review.

S.A.: Well, it's a tremendous piece of writing. We're all big fans of your writing, those of us who read you, and know you.

We'd crossed paths many times, but really, the Outlaw Bible is how we got connected for real.

Todd: The Outlaw Bible, it's still a fantastic piece of work.

S.A.: It's one helluva doorstop.

Todd: Yeah!

S.A. and Todd laugh…

S.A.: I could kick somebody's ass with it, shit.

Todd: Oh, yeah!

S.A.: The wrong person walks thru the door, I'll fuckin' whack 'em with it. I'll kick their ass with poetry!

Todd: You put that in a cloth bag and you'd probably beat the shit out of somebody.

S.A.: See, it has many practical uses. People who think that poetry has no practical use have no idea what they're talking about. It'll make short men tall.

Todd: And tall men short too!

S.A.: That's right! I'm trying to remember who turned you onto the Outlaw Bible. Was it Edward Field or Gerald Locklin?

Todd: No, it was Nelson Gary.

S.A.: That's right! And Nelson wrote that fantastic piece for you in there too.

Todd: Where is Nelson these days?

S.A.: Nelson is here right now. He is actually here even though we can't see him. Been talking to Nelson a lot the past few days, he's been spewing out some fine, fine poetry.

Todd: I'd say he's sort of out Marcel Prousted Proust!

S.A.: Now this is a question I had for you relative to the whole "outlaw" scene, it's kind of a chicken and egg routine. I know that you've been involved in this for a very long time, you've been writing Dillinger forever. In regards to the idea of actually naming this "outlaw poetry", whatever *this* is, did this have anything to do with The Outlaw Bible? Inspiring you in any way to fundamentally begin to set about the job of naming everything?

Todd: The Outlaw Bible sort of jump-started a whole bunch of stuff. That's right up on the table, that has to be admitted.

S.A.: I don't remember you ever discussing it in public that way before that. It's only been about the past five years or so you've been doing this.

Todd: Well, there's a real history here. In fact, I was cleaning my garage out about two years ago and came across a whole bunch of letters I had written to Tony Moffeit back in the early 80s. At that time, he and I were talking about outlaw poetry. From our talking about outlaw poetry, I published one of his early chapbooks called Outlaw Blues. So that sort of is, ya know, way back there. Of course, I'd been writing about outlaw stuff for a long time.

S.A.: Of course, you grew up in it.

Todd: Yeah. I was kind of calling it "noir poetry" for a long time. And then it came back around with The Outlaw Bible then in, what is it, '99, 2000?

S.A.: That's when it was published. I think you and I started talking in about '98. And we've talked about this much too; this thing really does come off the death of Jack Micheline, that's how the whole thing started. Literally does. Jack died, I wrote the eulogy, Kaufman read it and Kaufman and I began talking to each other.

I kind of assumed, that in part, that (The Outlaw Bible of American Poetry) had something to with inspiring you in some way to campaign, to create this school of poetics that you refer to as "outlaw poetry". Which especially a lot of younger guys, predictably so, some women involved too, but a lot of younger guys are really diggin' this, and are really listening to you, which is wonderful. You must be aware at this point, because it's gaining in popularity, the other thing's happening which almost validates the same thing; the naysayers, the people that think, "How could you possibly be outlaw? You're not robbing a fuckin' bank?" And that's fucking stupid, because that's not the point, not about the point at all.

Todd: No, that's way past the point.

S.A.: Of course it is.

Todd: Tony and I started talking about it again back in 2004. We started writing a bunch of manifestos back and forth, and emailing stuff. At the same time, I hooked up with my son Theron doing St. Vitus.

S.A.: And you've been doing St. Vitus since about what, 2001?

Todd: 2001. It was a hard copy for about five issues and then we decided to go online. One half of me wishes it was still hard copy in some ways, but then the other half of me says well it's available to a lot more people.

S.A.: I must say that in the realm of what might be outlaw poetry, nothing's more outlaw than the temporary feel of a book.

Todd: Hey, you got that right.

S.A.: You know what I'm saying? It's like you're holding the gun in your hand.

Todd: It's not romantic to take your laptop with you to bed, although I guess that some people do get off on it.

S.A.: Well, some people caress their laptops. I'm sure that they are right now. In fact, I just got a message, "My nipples are getting hard."

Todd: Oh, man!!! I'm feeling the vibes all over here!

Both laughing from the gut...

S.A.: I'm sorry; I undress. Okay, back to the outlaw thing. I know that people are listening and they do want to hear this.

Todd: So Tony and I wrote back and forth and we decided to hell with it, we'll just throw the dice against the wall and see what happens and just start the thing going. Start an outlaw movement. Part of it comes down to this, and I'm pretty sure you'll agree. If you look back in the last thirty, even forty years, where have the great poems gone? Where are the great poets? Except for Bukowski, who always was an outlaw unto himself anyway...

S.A.: He was the ultimate outlaw because he didn't belong anywhere.

Todd: Yeah. He didn't have to say he was an outlaw; he just was an outlaw.

S.A.: I agree.

Todd: Bukowski was a movement unto himself.

S.A.: Absolutely.

Todd: Besides him, if you look at the poetry world, both mainstream and small press, you don't find the giants of poetry after Olson and then after McGrath, McGrath was a real outlaw too, even though he was in academia.

S.A.: Philip Levine.

Todd: Well the thing about Levine that I like is that he had the feel for blue collar.

S.A.: He is blue collar, absolutely. He's Detroit, Fresno. He pretty much kept it real; he remained true to the muse.

Todd: Anyway, I thought, let's see if we can define outlaw poetry. See where that goes. That's what I've been playing with.

S.A.: So what do you think qualifies? How would you characterize it, actually define it? In as few words as you can, define outlaw poetry.

Todd: Oh, Christ...

S.A.: And you don't drink anymore.

Todd: And I could stand a couple of pints right here!

Outlaw poetry stands outside the whole thing. Outlaw poetry is the marginal poetry that is the central force of poetry today. It's people who've been marginalized. We've got a whole generation of small press poets who've been marginalized. There hasn't been one small press poet who's won the National Book Award, who has ever won the Pulitzer Prize, who has ever won the Walt Whitman Award — no small press poet.

RICK SMITH
Alta Loma, CA

Using Rain

No use buying
a used car
in the rain
in the night.
Any junker assumes
a showroom luster,
shines like zirconia.
No,
when it rains,
just
steal the damn car.

Glass breaking is
just a random gust,
shutters are
slaphappy in the wet wind.
A tree limb cracks
under the weight
of fresh water
and lands down the block.
Glass is best shattered
under cover of
hard rain.

Inside the storm
barely pausing for breath
you defy the liquid dark,
circle the wet streets.
There is the insistence
of pre-selected radio

and the glow of a red dial.
Hands are red
in the blurred
and private lighting,
red the hands
that hold
the wheel,
nothing
but the wheel.

* * *

Cotton Fever
(after Frank O'Hara)

Boxer floats in the Susquehanna,
one Everlast glove above the current.
He's fixed like a ram's head
in a Di Chirico,
pinned inside the screen.

Silver minnows
lean into all the hollows
and where he has been
is pure liquid.

The shooting gallery night
is poised for victims of the dance
but the soul skips away,
moves with the silver.

Dawn locates the new champion.
The light is soft,
the air still.

First appeared in Statement (1981)
and in revised form in Lungfull! (#18—2010)

C<small>APTAIN</small> B<small>AREFOOT</small>
Norwood, CO

**Not Homo Sapiens
But Humus Ludens***
—for Dillinger's Vergil

> Muddy tracks
> chasing that outlaw self
> rub dirt on us all.

*My Latin roots are showing up again; it's my name for our species, *humus ludens*... Not "Man thinking" but "Dust playing" — humus is dirt and ludere means to play — it's what we do best — sing, dance, tell stories. The whole point is that Todd took us into our outlaw shadow side, and as such helped us become more like dirt — more human...but rubbing something in the dirt usually means to make it more dirty and some would consider his outlaw poems obscene or thrill-seeking but I think he was exploring the violent nature of the American dream and making us more in touch with our essential human selves (as dust)...from dust we came and unto dust we will return. That's why I dedicate it to "Dillinger's *Vergil*"— since Publius Vergilius Maro was the bard who glorified Caesar Augustus — one of history's more famous "criminals"...

Capt. Barefoot

William Taylor, Jr.
San Francisco, CA

The Fire He Made
(For Todd Moore)

True outlaws live
lonely lives
and the man I am
thinking of
wandered through
this desert life
and made it
his own
spaghetti western
his own
pulp novel
his own
film noir
he was a tough
old boy
he'd gut you with a poem
like a Stanley knife
just as soon as look at you
he set the dark alight
with words like
firebombs he'd just
light the fuse and
keep walking
just because he could
and the fire he made
was so goddamned

pretty
you didn't care if
you were burning
he's gone now
he just wandered off
into the last
blazing sunset
having done what
he had come to do
though nobody much
ever thanked him
but that's the way
true outlaws go.

<u>G</u><u>LENN</u> <u>F</u><u>REY</u> & <u>D</u><u>ON</u> <u>H</u><u>ENLEY</u> (*THE EAGLES*)

DESPERADO

Desperado, why don't you come to your senses
You've been out ridin' fences,
for so long - now.
Ohh you're a hard one.
I know that you've got your reasons.
These things that are pleasin' you
Will hurt you somehow.

Don't you draw the queen of diamonds boy
She'll beat you if she's able.
You know the queen of hearts is always your best bet.
Now it seems to me, some fine things
Have been laid upon your table.
But you only want the ones
That you can't get.

Desperado,
Ohhhh you aint getting no younger.
Your pain and your hunger,
They're driving you home.
And freedom, ohh freedom.
Well that's just some people talking.
Your prison is walking through this world all alone.

Don't your feet get cold in the winter time?
The sky won't snow and the sun won't shine.
It's hard to tell the night time from the day.
And you're losing all your highs and lows
aint it funny how the feeling goes
away...

Desperado,
Why don't you come to your senses?
come down from your fences, open the gate.
It may be rainin', but there's a rainbow above you.
You better let somebody love you.
before it's too late.

RD ARMSTRONG
Long Beach, CA

AFTERWORD

IDON'T know how tough Todd Moore really was…a shot to the gut would've probably put him down for the count (owing to his condition and all); but I do know he was one helluva writer when it came to writing about tough guys & gals. Moore wrote mostly about Johnny Dillinger, the 30s gangster, America's Most Wanted for a couple of years and a real bad man. He also wrote about the various thugs and bad boys he heard about in his youth, growing up near Chicago's Southside in the 40s & 50s.

Unlike Bukowski, who wrote about everyday things and the way he dealt with them, Moore wrote about fantasy characters. Not only did he put himself in Dillinger's head & shoes and write a fantastic poem about Dillinger's life and times (a poem that lasted some 35 years), but he also put himself smack-dab in the middle of a world filled with violent encounters. Todd could do this, it was as if he was born to it, born to document the last moments of Dillinger's betrayal after being set up and shot in an alley behind the Biograph Theater in "The Corpse is Dreaming", a section from his epic Dillinger poem "My Name is Dillinger."

Unlike most poets, Todd didn't draw conclusions, or comment on the right or wrong of the subject he devoted his writing life to. He merely stated the facts: this happened, then this happened, then this happened…devoid of emotion…a sociopath reporting on a psychopathic world; hardly what you would expect from a well-read, mild-mannered English teacher & librarian.

I don't think he ever wrote about his life as a teacher and librarian, or being a family man, or raising two sons or being married to Barbara, his wonderful wife...if he did, he kept these to himself. It wouldn't be in keeping with the "Bad Boy" persona that he was developing.

When I first heard Todd speak, I remember thinking, 'this can't be THE Todd Moore, this guy sounds too timid.' And in the photo he sent me, he looked more like an insurance salesman than the guy who penned My Name is Dillinger. But then Truman Capote had a lisp and he wrote In Cold Blood...even Bukowski had a kind of an effeminate sounding voice and look at all the shit he wrote.

No, Moore had found his genre and was rapidly defining & refining it. I've read some of his earlier Dillinger sections and they lack the complexity of his later work. I think it's safe to say that during his last 20 years, Moore had honed his craft to razor sharpness. Unfortunately, while his last year appeared to be one of his best, there were events that would taint (and eventually spoil) our friendship. I should have seen the signs, but I was too caught up in the "mystique" that was Todd Moore. It is ironic that the humble writer I first met back in '97 could succumb to his own 'legend' – but these things happen. I doubt that Todd even noticed that he was starting to believe his own hype... something he had warned me about some ten years earlier.

He had told me then that when a poet starts worrying about his *legacy*, he'd better hang up his gloves, 'cause his days as a fighter were over. But, I guess it's easier to talk about them folks out there than it is to practice what you preach. As I said, I should have seen it coming.

I had plenty of chances during the "tour" we undertook in May of '09. We did five readings in 7 days in a grueling road trip that chalked up nearly 1200 miles. Todd and I had a lot of time to chat, though he did most of the talking and I did most of the listening. I should have noticed that Todd was pretty much in love with the sound of his own voice and really liked to preach the gospel according to Dillinger as interpreted by Todd Moore. At the same time, he assured me that I was doing him and other small press poets a major service by providing them with a forum from which to speak to the masses, something I've had my doubts about for the past few years as I've watched book sales drop, as well as the interest in books published by Lummox Press seemingly head towards zero. Perhaps my legacy is to publish the best books *never* read.

I don't know. But Todd was trying to buck up my spirits, which I greatly appreciated, since very few writers of his experience would bother to take the time. Perhaps they're all out there promoting their own legacy. Who can say? I know that publishing these books is my legacy as a publisher. I don't know if I have a legacy as a writer/poet. I know what I know, but I don't want to become one of these poets that go around constantly talking about how great their stuff is. Lord knows there are quite a few poets who do this...but I don't want to be like them.

Todd wrote about outlaws. It seems to be the thing for poets in the New Mexico/Colorado area (sort of the lore of the land). Not surprisingly he and Tony Moffeit came up with the Outlaw School of poetry, though some would say that it had its roots in the pretentious Outlaw Bible of American Poetry, one of the great cons of the last century. Todd was always trying to convince me that I was as *outlaw* as anybody that was in that book, but I never really bought it. I always figured that if you were an outlaw, the last thing you wanted to do was brag about it. To be honest, I am probably a lot more *outlaw* than Todd or anybody else in this movement knows about. Outlaw in practice, not just in speech or theory.

But that's not the point. The point is, I should have been listening closer to what Todd wasn't telling me, you know, the "sub" message. Maybe if I had, I could have alerted someone, or even gotten into trouble, as I often do for sticking my big nose into other people's business, telling Todd that he was starting to sound like a pompous ass and fulla shit, to boot. Of course, I don't think I could have ever said that, except in a fantasy poem, but the trouble is I had such a high respect for him that it bordered on fan worship; I was like a little girl worshiping Justin Bieber.. It was a "hard to see the forest for the trees" mindset.

The reader may be confused, since it would seem the editor and publisher of a tribute book for someone should be more supportive of a person's greatness and less picky about some of his shortcomings...and under most circumstances that would be the case; though, to be honest, in my last tribute book, "Last Call: The Legacy of Charles Bukowski," I wrote of Buk with the awareness that he was not all he was cracked up to be either.

My feeling is that to see a writer in all his or her complexity, one must allow the good and the not so good to be seen. There are many writers I wouldn't do a tribute book for, since, in my view, the 'not so good' far outweighs 'the good.' But in this case, as in the case of Buk, I think this writer was genuinely a good guy; besides being a good writer.

That said, I must acknowledge that this book is an 'unauthorized' edition. There has been a lot of "he said-she said" back-stabbing and veiled threats involved with my desire to publish this book. Certain parties have gone out of their way to 'control' the legacy of Todd's estate; even going so far as to prohibit the sale of Todd's books by any of the other small presses that have taken a chance on him. Of course this is bullshit of the highest order...but it's the wild and wooly small press, where anything goes, right? Ironically, the publication of this book adheres to the Outlaw tradition that Todd was promoting at the time of his death. I say ironic, because the persons who are trying to freeze out everyone else associated with Todd have threatened to sue anyone publishing unauthorized books about Todd...outlaws suing outlaws?

Isn't that ridiculous?

I admit that Todd and I did have a falling out about three months before he died, but I assumed that we would iron it out eventually. I didn't realize how bad things were with him, health-wise. It was some kind of misunderstanding, but I was surprised that the man who claimed I was his friend could drop me so nonchalantly. Todd had sent me a strange email just three months before his demise telling me not to publish anymore of his work (we had two more books set up, one of which included some of his many essays written for my now defunct Lummox Journal, which I was really looking forward to publishing). He was offended that I was "trying to make a buck" off of him and cheapen his image by offering his likeness on T Shirts, etc.

Apparently, he had thought I was just doing all this as a labor of love... nobody makes any money doing this, do they? I sure haven't been very successful at cashing in on any of the excellent writers I have published over the years, not even Mr. Todd Moore. But none of that matters now, does it?

So, without any fanfare, our communication of more

than a decade ended. And, needless to say, I found the whole thing pretty upsetting. I think I have done a pretty good job of presenting a fair and balanced view...in spite of the efforts of a certain party to sabotage potential contributors' participation telling them it would be against Todd's wishes for any of them to be associated with this project...

I have been advised to take the high road on this, but to be honest (as one who has taken this road before), while the high road has a lot of scenic vistas; it is a mighty lonesome place.

So here is my contribution to the 'lore' of Todd Moore; to the jumbled legacy of a man I once called friend. My adoration for him as a writer, is clearly represented by the poets and fans of his work that I have selected for this book. My personal conflict is represented here as well. I just hope that all sides will be weighed before the tar and feathering begins.

Photo by Pete Jonsson

BIOS

Michael Adams grew up in a steel town near Pittsburgh, Pennsylvania. He has a Bachelor's degree in Anthropology and a Master's degree in planning, both from the University of Pittsburgh. He attended the Jack Kerouac School of Disembodied Poetics at Naropa University in 1988. His latest book is *Steel Valley* (Lummox Press 2010). He performs poetry and music regularly with poets Phil Woods and James Taylor III and musician Jim Sheckells as the Free Radical Railroad. He lives in Lafayette, CO with his wife, Claire.

RD Armstrong aka *Raindog* has been lighting fires and biting tires for most of his life in the Los Angeles area. He has 18 chapbooks and 9 books to his name and has been published widely in print as well as on line. He also operates the Lummox Press which publishes the Little Red Book series and numerous perfect bound collections of poetry. For nearly 20 years, Raindog has labored to serve the world of small press poetry.

Captain Barefoot lives on the cusp of the Colorado Plateau and the Southern Rockies, where he grows heirloom seed potatoes and weaves baskets, while jousting with political windmills. He is a member of the Union of Street Poets, Vincent St. John Local and the Kuksu Brigade (retired).

Miles J. Bell is 39, and lives in England with his family. If anyone sees his muse, could you let him know - it's been gone a couple of years and he's beginning to wonder if it's ever coming back. Thank you.

E. R. Biggs lives near Santa Fe, NM with his dog. He edits *Rascals of the Red Barren Bar* and has three prose books. His poetry appears in Rascals, this volume, hundreds of web posts, and readings in the area. His fiction and nonfiction prose appears in two languages and several books.

Gary L. Brower is the editor of the Malpais Review, a director of the Duende Poetry Series of Placitas, has taught at various universities, and lives in Placitas, New Mexico.

Harry Calhoun grew up in Connellsville, a little town south of Pittsburgh. He snuck into Pittsburgh where he spent years as a bartender, article writer, poet and, finally, a marketing writer. He spent the mid-90s starving and doing poetry readings in Key West before relocating to Raleigh, North Carolina, where he has spent the past 15 years. He's been published in a ton of places, edits *Pig in a Poke* magazine, and has two books and two chapbooks published so far.

Alan Catlin has been in the small press poetry wars since the 70s; from the mimeos to cyberspace. His latest book is *"Near Death in the Afternoon on Becker Street"* from March Street Press.

John Dorsey currently resides in Toledo Ohio. His work has appeared in fearless, Spent Meat, James River Poetry Review, Typewriter Voodoo, Out of Order, and Mystery Island Magazine, as well as the recent collections, *"Little Boy Beat: Selected Poems"*, and

"The Dusty and Lofty Dreams of Middle Class Fairy Princesses."

Hugh Fox lives in East Lansing, Michigan, retired after teaching English/American Lit/Film for 50 years. Latest book is *WHERE SANITY BEGINS* from Cervena Barva Press in Somerville. Fighting prostate cancer. Two major surgeries. Has had one of Todd's poems (signed to him) on the wall in front of his computer for the last thirty years.

Nelson Gary's most recent book is *Twin Volumes* (Ethelrod Press). It is his fourth book. Nelson Gary's poetry and prose have also been published in *The Outlaw Bible of American Poetry* (Thunder's Mouth Press).

Elliott Gorn teaches American history at Brown University. He is author of *Dillinger's Wild Ride: The Year that Made America's Public Enemy Number One,* as well as works on boxers, labor organizers, frontier fighters, and other outlaws. He lives in Providence, but his heart is in Chicago.

Gary Goude has been involved with the small press for nearly 20 years. He has been published in numerous journals including *The Wormwood Review, The New York Quarterly* and *Twisted Savage.* His titles include *The Killing Time, Looking With Bleeding Eyes for the Tiger,* and *Blood on Blood* w/ Todd Moore. He still lives in Riverside, CA.

S. A. Griffin lives, loves and works in Los Angeles. Recent titles include *They Swear We Don't Exist, Numbskull Sutra* and *Greatest Hits.* Editor, *The Outlaw Bible of American Poetry.* April-June

2010 toured the U.S. on his *Poetry Bomb Couch Surfing Across America Tour of Words*, promoting education, community and disagreements. S.A. lives in Los Angeles with his wife Lorraine.

Brent Leake lives in Salt Lake City. He works in the social justice field....reinventing justice through alternatives to incarceration. He's been writing poetry since the late 60s. Recent titles include *The Hell Hounds Come Howling*, Pentatonic *Poetry In The Key Of Blues* and *Blues From The Graybar Hotel*. His music has appeared on various Zerx cd's

Father Luke waits with the woman he loves for a perfect world. He lives in Portland, Oregon. He may be reached at http://FatherLuke.com

John Macker lives in Northern New Mexico with artist wife Annie. Recently published *Underground Sky*. Previously, *Woman of the Disturbed Earth* and *Las Montanas de Santa Fe*, with woodcuts by Leon Loughridge.

Ann Menebroker has been publishing since the late 1950s. Her work can be found in chapbooks, collected poems, anthologies, textbooks, and in a storage unit she keeps, since moving into a small apartment in Dec of 2010. The latest book, *Sunscreen in the Fog*, was published by Bottle of Smoke Press in 2010.

Tony Moffeit lives, writes, and sings the blues in Pueblo, Colorado. Along with Todd Moore, he co-founded the outlaw poetry movement. His books include *Poetry Is Dangerous: The Poet Is an Outlaw* (featuring essays, as well as poems) and *Pueblo Blues*

(winner of the Jack Kerouac Award from Cherry Valley Editions).

Biola Olatunde, poet, dramatist and novelist lives and writes from Akure, Ondo state in Nigeria. She has in the works a collection of poems: "Memories of a forgotten slumber." Some poems of hers were accepted on the *OUTLAW POETRY NETWORK* including "She was Twelve" & "There's a saying." She has a novel about the Niger Delta in her country coming out soon.

Orion is a poet, video artist, and singer who currently lives in Alaska. He is the author of *Honky Tonk Heroes*, a poetry tribute to Waylon Jennings and Willie Nelson, published in 2009.

Niall O'Sullivan has performed poetry at venues, theatres and festivals all over the UK and Europe since the late nineties. He has published two full collections of poetry with flipped eye, the latest being 2007's *Ventriloquism for Monkeys* from which the poem 'The Father in Law' was highly commended by the 2008 Forward Prize judges. Niall featured on BBC Radio and Television during his residency at the 2009 Wimbledon Tennis Championships. He currently hosts Poetry Unplugged, London's biggest open mic, at Covent Garden's Poetry Café and teaches at the Poetry School.

Joe Pachinko was born and raised in Oakland CA. The author of a novel, *"SWAMP!"*, also *"The Urinals of Hell"* & *"Stumpfucker Cavalcade"*, poetry; his new novel, *"Geek City Apocalypso"* should be out soon.

David S. Pointer was the son of a bank robber. David

also served with the Marine military police. He's not quite sure how he got mixed up with Todd and Theron Moore over at St. Vitus Press.

Casey Quinn has had over 250 poems published in print or online venues. His second poetry chapbook *Prepare to Crash* was released in 2009 by Big Table Publishing. His third book will be released in 2011 by Epic Rites Press. In his free time he edits *Short Story Library magazine.*

Misti Rainwater-Lites is responsible for bullshit rodeo, bunny man and numerous other literary extravagances.

Ben Smith is a Melbourne based writer who runs a literary porno web site, www.horrorsleazetrash. com. He was once a model in a queer magazine but is convinced he is as straight as an arrow. He never met Todd but he misses him. Some people leave voids in the world when they go, while everyone else just get carved in 'em.

Rick Smith is a clinician psychologist specializing in brain damage and domestic violence. He plays harmonica and writes songs for The Mescal Sheiks (see mescalsheiks.com). Poems have appeared in Water-Stone, OnTheBus, New Letters, Spillway, South Bay Magazine...Most recent book is *Hard Landing* (Lummox Press, 2010)

Joe Speer lived and traveled in a 1977 VW camper. He attended open mic nights to share his stories and poems. Along with Pamela Hirst, they published Beatlick News and hold a presence on the web at www.beatlick.com. They were planning to spend winters in Mexico, until Joe's untimely death in January, 2011.

Belinda Subraman is a poet, writer, filmmaker, podcaster, artist, traveler and registered nurse. Working on a novel. Latest poetry book is *BLUE ROOMS, BLACK HOLES, WHITE LIGHTS.* http://www.BelindaSubraman.com

William Taylor, Jr. lives in San Francisco with a lovely wife and a lovely cat. His latest collection of poetry is *The Hunger Season* (Sunnyoutside, 2009). He recently co-edited, along with RD Armstrong, *Down This Crooked Road: Modern Poetry From the Road less Traveled* (Lummox, 2009). *An Age of Monsters,* his first collection of prose is due out in 2011 from Epic Rites Press.

Mark Weber is a jazz disc jockey who lives in Albuquerque. Spin the cosmic world wide web dial to KUNM.org Thursday afternoons or terrestrially at 89.9FM to hear him.

Patricia Wellingham-Jones is published in many anthologies, journals and Internet magazines, including HazMat Review, Ibbetson Street, Edgz and Wicked Alice. She has a special interest in healing writing and writes for the review department of Recovering the Self: a journal of hope and healing. Poetry chapbooks include *Don't Turn Away: poems about breast cancer, End-Cycle: poems about caregiving, Apple Blossoms at Eye Level, Voices on the Land* and *Hormone Stew.*

Lawrence Welsh has published seven books of poetry, including *Skull Highway* (La Alameda Press, 2008)

and *Carney Takedown* (Unlikely Books, 2010).
A new collection, *Begging for Vultures: New and Selected Poems, 1994-2009*, will be published in 2011 by the University of New Mexico Press. Welsh is an associate professor of English at El Paso Community College. In 1979, Welsh co-founded *The Alcoholics*, the Los Angeles punk rock band. Next year, Artifix Records of Southern California will release *The Alcoholics: East of Sepulveda, 1979-82*, a retrospective of the band's studio and live cuts.

Neal Wilgus lives in Corrales, New Mexico with his son. His reviews and interviews have been widely published in the small press in mags like Small Press Review. He has also written a few books.

Don Winter Between 1999 and 2008, Don Winter's poems appeared in most small press, and many academic press journals.

F. N. Wright lives in the coastal mountains of southern California. He is the author of 4 novels and several poetry chapbooks including *Piss On The Pope*.

Anita L. Wynn, born Nov. 5, 1963, and wrote reams of bad poems before she grew into herself. She raised two strong, intelligent young men. She went to college at the University of Georgia. She published three books: Speaking in Tongues, by Autolykos (PublishAmerica); White Horses, (PublishAmerica); and Bare Feet, Broken Glass, (Lummox Press).

Scot Young lives in Missouri.

A NEAR-COMPLETE BIBLIOGRAPHY OF
TODD MOORE TITLES & RECORDINGS

The Man in the Black Chevrolet (Duck Down Press) 1976
The Dillinger Poems (Uzzano) 1978
The Name is Dillinger: Book two (Midwestern Writers Pub.) 1980
Driving 1980
Aces + Eights (Crawlspace Press) 1981
The Dark and Bloody Ground 1981
D.O.A. (Crawlspace Press) 1983
Point Blank (Black Mask Press) 1983
America in Pictures 1984
Dead Center 1985
Tough Ass 1985
Two Poems from Scales and Weights 1985
Target Practice 1985
Watching / The Wormwood Review #98 1985 (mag.)
Blood on the Moon (Chawed Rawzin Press) 1985
The Name is Dillinger Vol. 1 (Kangaroo Court Press) 1986
Dillinger's Faces Vol. 2 (Kangaroo Court Press) 1986
Dillinger: Billie F Vol. 3 (Kangaroo Court Press) 1987
Drunk at the Movies 1987
Todd Moore 1987
Poetry Motel #10 1987
Take No Prisoners 1987
Afraid He'd (No Press) 1987
Poetry Eclectic (Electric Press) 1988
Playing Poker W/ .22 Longs (Persona Non Grata Press) 1988
Shallow Graves 1989
6 Poems (Speakeasy Pub.) 1989

Dillinger's Keys 1989

Dillinger Let 1989

Dillinger (Lobo Press) 1990

More Moore (Vergin Press) 1990

First Switchblade 1990

Night in the Blood w/ Dennis Gulling 1990

The Taste of Blood 1991

Dillinger and the Color Red 1991

TODD MOORE PACKS IT IN (Zerx Press)1992

I Want A Poem to Be Hard Like A Bullet 1992

Boneyard 1992

The Last Good Thing (Bull Thistle Press) 1993

Shooting out the Lights / Swindler's Harmonica Siesta
    w/Mark Weber (Zerx Press) 1994

Dancing w/ Blood 1994

Driveby 1994

Machine Gun (Crawlspace Press) 1994

Shooting Out the Lights 1994

American Cannibal 1994

Dead Run 1995

Weapon of Choice 1995

White Boy Meets Dillinger (Concrete Block In Your Face
    Then Press) 1995

Dreaming with Bones 1996

Death, Glory, Sequins and Smoke 1996

A Hotel Education 1997

The Rat's Blood Had Glued My Hand Shut 1997

Some Die Along the Way 1997

Wolf Mask 1997

The Lummox Journal, intermittently from 1997 to 2006
    (2 interviews, 13 or so essays, numerous poems) (mag.)

Solo #2 1998 (mag.)

Bone w/ RD Armstrong (Lummox Press) 1999

Shotgun Blues (Phony Lid Pubs)1999

Working on my Duende (Kings Estate Press) 1999

The Corpse is Dreaming (Lummox Press) 2000

Bombed in New Mexico w/ Mark Weber (Lummox Press) 2000

Dead Eye 2001

Dillinger's Thompson (Phony Lid Press) 2002

The First One Hurt 2003

Dark Red Candy 2003

Snub; A Collection of Poetry 2003

The Weather in Hell (Spankstra Press) 2004

Last Call: The Legacy of Charles Bukowski (Lummox Press) 2004

Russian Roulette / Sign of the Gun (Spankstra Press) 2005

The Dead Zone Trilogy (St. Vitus Press) 2005

The Desert Shovel Review #1 2006 (mag.)

An Interview with Todd Moore by Neal Wilgus 2006

Outlaw 2006

Blood on Blood w/ Gary Goude (St. Vitus Press) 2006

Shotgun Weather w/ Dennis Gulling (St. Vitus Press) 2007

Love & Death & Teeth in the Blood (Pitchfork Press) 2007

Tell the Corpse A Story (Bill Crane's Books) 2008

Blind Whiskey & The Straight Razor Blues (Iniquity Press) 2008

Relentless (Bill Crane's Books) 2009

Dead Reckoning (Epic Rites Press) 2009

The Riddle of the Wooden Gun (Lummox Press) 2009

The Long Way Home (Lummox Press) 2009

The Gunfighter Elegies 2010

Malpais Review w/others 2010 (mag.)

RECORDINGS

Poetry Reading Nov. 11, 1989

Long Sections of Dillinger (cassette)1995

Dillinger 1999

Dillinger (Zerx #039, double CD) 2001

Todd Moore CD 2001

Albuzerxque Vol. 12 (Zerx CD) 2002

Albuzerxque Vol. 17 (Zerx CD) 2004

Albuzerxque Vol. 18 (Zerx) 2004

Albuzerxque Vol. 22 (Zerx) 2006

Style: A Todd Moore Interview DVD 2006

Todd Moore Reads. Recorded in Magdalena, NM
    VOX Audio by Bruce Holapple, 2006

The Blue Dragon Café Reading 2006

Albuzerxque Vol. 27 (Zerx) 2007

Todd Moore CD 2007

Todd Moore CD 2007

Mera Wolf and Todd Moore Read at Acequia Booksellers in
    Albuquerque, NM, *VOX Audio by Bruce Holapple, 2008*

Todd Moore and Lawrence Welsh Read at Acequia
    Booksellers, *VOX Audio by Bruce Holapple, 2009*

Memorial Reading for Todd Moore at the Harwood Art
    Center, Albuquerque, NM, *VOX Audio by Bruce
    Holapple, 2010*

TODD MOORE Remembered

TODD MOORE

THE RIDDLE OF THE WOODEN GUN

Published in 2009 by Lummox Press

ABOUT THE LUMMOX PRESS

LUMMOX PRESS was created in 1994 by RD Armstrong. It began as a self-publishing/DIY imprint for poetry by RD. Several chapbooks were published and in late 1995 it began publishing the *LUMMOX Journal*, a monthly small/underground press lit-arts mag. Available primarily by subscription, the *LJ* continued its exploration of the "creative process" until its demise as a print mag in 2006. It was hailed as one of the best monthlies in the small press.

In 1998, Lummox began publishing the Little Red Book series, and continues to do so today. To date there are some 59 titles in the series (as of 2010) and a collection of poems from the first decade of the series has been published under the title, The Long Way Home (2009); it's a great way to explore the series.

Together with Chris Yeseta (Layout and Art Direction since 1997), RD continues to publish books that are both striking in their looks as well as their content…you'd think he was aping Black Sparrow, but he is merely trying to produce the best books he can for his clients, the poets, and their customers, you, the readers.

* * *

The following books are available directly from the Lummox Press via its website: **www.lummoxpress.com** or at Lummox, c/o PO Box 5301, San Pedro, CA 90733. There are also E-Book (PDF) versions of most titles available. Most of these titles are available through other book sellers online, as well.

The Wren Notebook by Rick Smith (2000)

Last Call: The Legacy of Charles Bukowski
    edited by RD Armstrong (2004)

On/Off the Beaten Path by RD Armstrong (2008)

Fire and Rain—Selected Poems 1993-2007,
    Volumes 1 & 2 by RD Armstrong (2008)

El Pagano and Other Twisted Tales by RD Armstrong
    (short stories—2008)

New and Selected Poems by John Yamrus (2009)

The Riddle of the Wooden Gun by Todd Moore (2009)

Sea Trails by Pris Campbell (2009)

Down This Crooked Road – Modern Poetry from the
    Road Less Traveled edited by RD Armstrong and
    William Taylor, Jr. (2009)

The Long Way Home Ten Years of the Little Red Book
    Series edited by RD Armstrong (2009)

Drive By by John Bennett (2010)

Modest Aspirations by Gerald Locklin & Beth Wilson
    (2010)

Steel Valley by Michael Adams (2010)

Hard Landing by Rick Smith (2010)

A Love Letter to Darwin by Jane Crown (2010)

E / OR—Living Amongst the Mangled by RD
    Armstrong (2010)

Ginger, Lily & Sweet Fire A Romance with Food
    by H. Lamar Thomas (2010)

Whose Cries Are Not Music by Linda Benninghoff
    (2011)

Dog Whistle Politics by Michael Paul (2011)

Working the Wreckage of the American Poem
    edited by RD Armstrong (2011)

What Looks Like an Elephant by Edward Nudleman
    (2011)

www.ingramcontent.com/pod-product-compliance
Lightning Source LLC
Chambersburg PA
CBHW051834090426
42736CB00011B/1804